ECHOES

TIRED, WORN OUT & OVER IT.
IGNORING THE ECHOES & LISTENING TO GOD'S VOICE

The repetitions of my past echoed in my soul…
and led me to the melodic life-giving heartbeat of what remained.

by

Stephanie D. Moore

Moore Marketing and Communications
Oklahoma City, Oklahoma
www.StephanieDMoore.com

Bulk copies or group sales of this book are available by contacting moore@stephaniedmoore.com or by calling (405) 248-7038.

FIRST EDITION PRINTED MARCH 2015
Printed in USA

Moore, Stephanie D.
Echoes: Tired, Worn Out & Over It. Ignoring the Echoes & Listening to God's Voice – First edition.

Issued also as an ebook.

ISBN: 978-0-9962040-7-1

This book is dedicated to my mom...
who never stopped praying for me.

Special Thanks

Mom & Dad
Dallas, Brooklyn & Kaylia Moore
Levi Crawford
Percy, Jessica, Joseph, Matthew, Matthias, Bethany
Peabody & Bertha Bradley
DeLores & Percy Smith
Keith, Lillie & Larry Moore
Bradley Family
Smith Family
Rishelle Milton & Family
Reverend B.W. Noble
Pastor Charles Odom
Minister Kim Johnson
Mikenda Early
Delmar Johnson
Yaisa Mann

Last but not least,
Keeper-Catran Whitney
who inspired me to write this book.

I remember being young enough not to understand what was happening and old enough to understand what was. I'd heard my mother yelling at my father on the yellow stationary handset phone with the coiled up cord stretching from the kitchen wall down into her bedroom. Memories of my uncle getting on the call cussing my dad out for making my mother cry with his insensitive words… that I couldn't hear but knew they were ugly enough to make the entire household of his siblings angry... quickly rushed in.

My parents were getting a divorce. I can clearly see the 'Evel Kanevil' book my dad had given my brother and I after his long "road trip" prior to he and mom asking us if we knew what a "divorce" meant. I knew… and instantly my eyes welled up with tears. This was worse than the day my parent's had to break the news to me that I wasn't white. I was different. Even though every other kid in my class was white, I was not. I was different. I remember feeling like they were telling me I wasn't good enough. The way "different" was expressed made me feel like it meant something bad. All I wanted were Chinese bangs that I could blow up in the air like the other little girl in my class. She had pretty hair and everyone admired her, but she hated me… and I hated me… and that's how this made me feel. Like the family my dad created was no longer good enough for him…like we were "different".

Yes, I knew what divorce meant. It meant that my parents weren't in love anymore, and the small semblance of family we were used to… was going to soon fade away. It also meant my brother, new baby sister and I were moving from a beautiful hog farm full of acreage and plenty of places for a child to run wild and play to the cold streets of the projects where winos and drug addicts seem to wander aimlessly without concern. I'd never been to Oklahoma, I'd spent all my days in Pennsylvania. I had no idea culture shock equivalent to taking an unexpected ice bucket challenge would embrace me at first sight, but I did know that it meant my daddy wasn't coming with us. He was the first man that walked away… and his footsteps still have a faint echo in my soul.

*This book will tell the careful story of one woman's journey through the wilderness of molestation, gang violence, rape, drug addiction, homelessness and lost love to the promised land of wholeness, success, professional victory and peace. **The art of life is not listening to the echo of things lost, but hearing the melodic steady and consistent life-giving heartbeat of what remains.***

Chapter 1

In Love with My Molester

When we were young, my grandmother passed away due to heart issues one summer. Soon after, my family had to move in with my grandfather. In our house, it was my grandpa, my mom, my brother, my baby sister, my uncles and me. We lived on a beautiful farm out in the country. My grandfather raised hogs. The hog pen sat at the top of a large grassy hill. It stunk to high heaven and I only went up there when I had too!

A Beautiful Place

We had Weeping Willow trees that lined our acreage like a safety fence. They were tall and humongous. The best resting was done on the soft grassy knolls beneath those trees as the billowy branches hung down to cover me in shade. I loved those trees, they were gorgeous and majestic.

On the farm, living was quiet and peaceful (at least most of the time). On a good day, my mom would tell us to grab a plastic bowl and come with her which usually created all types of excitement. We knew we were on our way to the beautiful and full blackberry bushes. The fruit was so succulent, all you had to do was rinse them off and add a little sugar! We also grew corn and green beans and some other vegetables up the street from our house.

My grandfather had a gigantic junkyard behind the house. It was full of magic with much to explore. We weren't allowed back there often because it was dangerous. There was an abandoned school bus, junk cars and tons of other junk you could get into. Our driveway was created of those red acme bricks... the kind that had different text inscribed on each one. I enjoyed reading those bricks! They were very interesting to me for some reason despite just having cities and years and other boring information printed on them.

In the winter, it would snow – a lot. I remember the snow going so high that it came up the steps and into the middle of our front door. Our house wasn't majestic, it was simple with a two story garage big enough to fit two cars with a loft above for washing clothing or a make shift bedroom. We had a large living room, sitting room and 2 bedrooms. In one bedroom my uncles and brother slept, in the other my grandfather and I. My mom and little sister slept in the sitting room. My dad wasn't there much at all. He was always working or on tour with a music group.

A Great Man of Stature and Strength

My grandpa was a handsome man. He was large in stature, strong, light-skinned with peppered black curly hair and a huge smile. He was the rock of the family. I remember sleeping at the foot of his bed and feeling safe with grandpa around. He protected and spoiled me rotten. He had a way of making me feel so important, loved and welcome in his life. It's important for a young lady to feel welcome in her father's life. It lets her know she is loved. He always gave me whatever I wanted. I remember him cooking for my brother and I. He was the first person to turn us on to rice with toast butter and sugar. I think he loved to cook. He would always call us in the kitchen and clearly instruct us to sit down to eat. We always prayed over our food. He taught me how to shuck corn, snap peas and to make homemade ice cream. He was a hard-working man that was full of love.

I remember my grandpa waking up early in the morning. He was always busy making money to support us. His list of duties seemed endless... from selling scrap metal from his junk yard to selling hogs and doing only God knows what else... I was too young to know but he never stopped working. On his breaks he would hang out with my brother and I.

A Wonderful Family

My dad has three brothers who are charismatic and strong. My oldest uncle moved to pursue music dreams in Atlanta, but the younger two were still home. The youngest, was really playful and I connected with him most. He was very funny and liked to play tricks on us all the time. When my grandmother was alive I remember her throwing shoes at him all the time for his playful ways and smart-alecky mouth. My older uncle was quiet, friendly and reserved. He had a really sweet smile and wouldn't hurt a fly. They both loved video games, music, football and girls!

I really looked up to them even though I swear they paid me no mind. I loved to play outside. I always wanted to be a cheerleader, so that is what I did most often, create cheers. I was always determined to get their attention… somehow. But they were in high school and it seemed like all they thought about were girls! That is all they talked about… besides the Pittsburgh Steelers, high school drama or the Atari. They were sociable guys and always had friends coming over too.

My brother and I were best friends. We are 11 months apart but seemed to experience a lot of things at the same time. We were in most of our classes together and often shared the same group of friends. We shared everything from sandwiches to toys to shoes. You name it we shared it. He was my partner in crime when he wasn't hanging out with my uncles. He loved to follow them around and mimic what they did. He loved living on the farm as much as I did. My baby sister was just too dang little to play with. She was still an infant, 2 or 3 months old. She was adorable, cuddly and cute!

My mom worked a lot. She worked a couple of places, but the most memorable by far was Baskin Robbins! We ate ice cream cake on the holidays and occasionally she brought home ice cream. She loved us but life was kicking her in the booty. In hind sight, living so far from your family, with your in-laws while your husband was out working/possibly cheating… couldn't have been fun. It was hard to really process how she felt and to really know what my perception of it was.

Even though my dad wasn't around, I love him greatly. Before we moved in with grandpa, he was always around. He was a photographer and a musician. He always took tons of pictures of us and developed them in his development room. He watched movies with us and took us to the movies often. He is a really intelligent, caring and loving man.

Trick-or-Treat?

I was 8-years old and it was around Halloween. I'd recently went on an amazing trip with the Girl Scouts. We rode in the back of a pickup truck all the way up a curvy hill, laughing and singing. We went to a bon fire and bobbed for apples… it was a tremendous amount of fun. We sang Old Smokey and ate tons of candy. I will never forget it.

I loved the holidays, especially at school. We were allowed to create different Halloween crafts and use Halloween stories in our homework. It was an exciting time. At home, we always watched all the scary movies.

Later that month, my brother and I were dressed for Halloween. We begged and begged my uncles to take us trick-or-treating with them. They insisted they were way too old to trick-or-treat and that is something they wouldn't be doing with us. My brother and I were dressed up and went along our merry way. I imagine my mother took us because I can't really remember the details all too well. What I do remember is what happened later that night.

When we got home, my uncles had two gigantic pillowcases and politely informed us that they changed their mind and were now going trick-or-treating. Their adopted friend from up the street came. He was dressed like Doc of Prince and the Revolution. He was really cute. He had pretty wavy long hair and really light skin. I am not sure if he was white or multi-racial, regardless, I thought he was the most beautiful thing walking.

He Must Have Thought The Same Thing About Me

The friend that dressed as Doc was a close friend of my older uncle. They hung out almost every day. I was just a kid going on 25. One day when my dad was home, he and my mom were watching Purple Rain. The movie was very popular. I would dance around the house singing those songs and every now and again I noticed my uncle's friend watching me.

I don't remember what day it started, but I do remember the first time my uncle's friend asked me to sit next to him on the couch in the living room. When I sat down, he moved me closer. He always wanted me to sit right next to him on the couch.

He smiled at me and told me how beautiful I was...that I had pretty eyes and beautiful lips. He told me that he wanted to show me something. He took my hand and put it in his pants. He asked me if I could feel that it was growing. He told me it was because he was falling in love with me. That I was the most beautiful girl he'd ever met. I'd heard people on television talk like this before, but no one ever talked to me like that. He kept making me stroke him until he came. I remember looking down at my Barbie and Ken dolls trying to process it all.

Around my uncles, their friend ignored me. He acted like he couldn't see me. I would still do cheers, play games and try to have fun. But, something was different. My grades began to fail and he became more aggressive. Eventually, my hands weren't enough he wanted me to kiss it… to taste him. To show him how much I loved him back. The more he ignored me when they were around, the more I gave him when we were together.

I don't exactly know why I wanted his attention so much. Maybe it was because he was an adult that wanted to spend time with just me. My parents were fighting, my mom working and taking care of my baby sister, my grandpa working, my uncles chasing girls -

being teenagers and my brother chasing them... I almost think I wanted or needed his love and attention.

Before long, he began to penetrate me. At first with Barbie doll legs or brush handles, but after I would sit on his lap. He made quiet noises...

I remember my male cousins coming over. I thought I was so smart and sexy. Yes, I was sexy now. I was a woman and no one could tell me I wasn't. I wanted to show them I understood life. So I would take them out back and kiss them and let them touch me. I would *teach* them to touch me. I was spiraling out of control and no one knew a thing about it to care...

As Quickly As It Began, It Ended... Abruptly And Swiftly

Suddenly my parents were talking to us about divorce and told my brother and I we were moving. My secret love affair was over. We were moving back to Oklahoma where my mom's family lived.

In hindsight, I often found it ironic that I lived in a house full of men that loved me but somehow still couldn't be protected. My uncles were heavily into girls and my grandpa would watch this football show on a cable network and it seemed like that show was always about sex. He would always have me turn around during the bad parts, but as I understood it was really about sex more than football. My mom was working all the time. I only had life and TV to tell me. So, I assumed women were created for sex.

Similarities between the relationship blue print my molester gave me and the relationship blueprint my father provided were that a man could only secretly be in love. A man's actions nor his deeds mirrored the promises made.

The footsteps I heard walk away as we left for Oklahoma echoed loudly. They were the footsteps of my dad, my grandpa, my uncles and my molester whom I had grown to love fiercely.

Chapter 2

Ol' Wagonhead

My mom has the largest family I have ever seen! Her mom had eleven kids and my great grandmother had 16 children including an adoption and those that passed at birth. They grew up in the country too, but it was far different from Pennsylvania. This country was dusty, full of gravel, horses and four runners! They also picked cotton for pay… I remember one of my uncles told me they would earn a dollar per 1 pound bag they picked. He managed to fill two bags at a time.

I had no idea how big my mom's family actually was until we moved to Oklahoma. I could never imagine being in a family so large!

My mom had ten brothers and sisters, mostly brothers… seven of them to be exact. There were two sets of twins (one female set and one male set – the boys came last) and my mom was the oldest girl. Each of my uncles has different personalities, but in general they were similar in beliefs, responsibility, power and strength.

I also have a million cousins. When we first moved here, I heard one of my younger cousins tell my grandpa, "They talk funny". They all laughed at my brother and I because we supposedly had an accent. We had so many cousins and family it was hard to keep track. But it was a whole lot of fun. Just imagine inheriting 12-15 new friends in less than a week… that is what it felt like!

My grandfather and grandmother moved out of the country and into a small city. They were considered pillars within the community. They owned their own cab stand. At one point in time, my grandfather had been a sergeant or lieutenant on the police force and my grandmother beyond bearing 11 children, worked more than 25 years at the local hospital. Now they owned this cab stand that once belonged to my grandfather's dad.

I could easily remember my grandparents always drove the nicest Lincoln or Cadillac offered. It would always be lined with the gold trim and fabric top, leather seats and nice rims. My grandmother always kept a .22 pistol in the glove compartment because she wore a lot of jewelry and always had a lot of cash in the car making deposits for the cab stand. Their home was always clean and full of food. They made sure each of us grandkids not only attended church each Sunday but were dressed and ready for Sunday school. Each of us always worked some position in the church. We were all in the choir, drill team and attended every Baptist convention possible.

My grandmother also made sure we knew how to count and sort money. She was good with money. Her entire career she placed 50% of her checks into savings bonds. It was the responsibility of my brother and me to sort the cash and change they would get at the cab stand. We would clean my grandmother's house to earn money and would love to sit over there and watch TV.

My grandfather was blind. He wasn't born that way but it

happened later on in life when he worked as a park ranger… he was lifting a cement table top and suddenly, it happened. He could still see shadows and was one of the funniest men I knew. Boy, could he talk. I remember my grandmother constantly tugging at the arm of his jacket in Sunday school to let him know… he was rambling.

Sowing a Seed

Of my seven uncles, the oldest stepped in and became a surrogate father to my siblings and me. He made sure to come and get us on every birthday. We knew he would bring a set of clothing, a crisp ten dollar bill and take us to get something to eat —no matter what. In the summer, he would take us to his house to spend the night and play games and the next day he would take us to Showbiz Pizza and the Tulsa Zoo. He did that each summer… things we imagined a father would do. He loved us so much and allowed his actions to speak louder than his words.

When we saw him sitting on the porch, he would always call us, "Ol' Wagonhead" or "What you doing wagonhead?" He was a jolly man with a big smile surrounded by big lips. He was light skinned and wore those tinted prescription glasses and a loose jerry curl. He would sit on the bench on my grandmother's porch and watch us play. He always protected us through cautionary tales and made sure we were doing well in school.

He was definitely the oldest brother, as all of my other uncles respected and admired him. I would love to hear him talk mess to them as they slapped dominoes down on the table in record speed. If any man hesitated, he would bellow, "Study long, study wrong." To which would quickly be followed by laughter and other bantering remarks from around the room.

Years later, we visited my grandmother's house and they told us he was sick. He was very sick. You see he worked for a glass company for years, and the I believe the chemicals they used in that place gave him cancer (or some terminal illness). I watched as he became weaker and weaker. Then one day, they moved him into a bed that was in my grandmother's dining room. The table and chairs were removed. All that remained was the bookshelf that was lined with encyclopedias, cookbooks, bible books and college books; and a beautiful glass china cabinet that housed good china that we would never use. In the dining room, my uncle would be close to my grandfather. I imagine the wonderful talks they must have enjoyed during his last days. My grandfather had a favorite recliner in the living room where he could hear television. The dining room is very close by and well, thinking about it, I imagine it is exactly what my grandfather asked for. He was that type of man. He was simply a good man that couldn't imagine his oldest son dying before himself. A man who didn't want to let go of his first child... yes, I imagine it was very hard for him.

I remember when my uncle passed away. As the soldiers folded a flag in his honor that was to be placed on his coffin I could hear my grandfather sobbing loudly, seated in his chair...in front of that grave. He cried and cried and while he was a strong man amongst six of his strong sons and plenty of strong men he mentored in the community, he cried without shame for the loss of his oldest son.

In this memory, I hear the echoes of my uncle's laughter, taunting and caring spirit and the harsh reality of my grandfather sobbing for his oldest son before his grave.

Chapter 3

Fear, Sex, Gangs and Death

Freshman Year

It was my freshman year, and I was growing into the body of a beautiful young woman. My shape felt like a figure-eight (even with a little weight on me). My walk had a hypnotic sway and I had a grace about me that was seemingly irresistible (if you let me tell it). I was beginning to get a lot of attention. The boys I went to school with were out of control and relentless. Most of them hoped I would be willing to do what I was too fearful of even considering. I loved the admiration... but I hated it at the same time. For one, I was deathly afraid of boys. For two, the other girls seemed to hate me for it.

Most teens are so convinced they are adults... they hate any boundary that isn't self-inflicted. But I wasn't a normal teen, I'd seen first-hand what crossed boundaries resulted in. My experience with molestation influenced me in ways I didn't even realize. I was not only no longer in love with my molester, but I began to hate myself and the things I did... even if they weren't my fault. I swear from the outside looking in it would seem as though I was a bit bi-polar because I teeter-tottered between absolutely loving myself AND hating everything about me. I often felt ugly, unworthy and depressed... despite all of the attention I received. Most days, teenage boys or grown men would follow me and try to talk to me especially after school. It scared me. I don't know why but I never thought there was genuine interest… and it didn't matter if I was going to wash clothes, taking out the trash or checking the mail, they were everywhere.

I remember one boy cornered me in the arcade at the mall. He was handsome and he was sweet but I was afraid. I had no idea what being someone's girlfriend meant! My cousin that was with me called me 7 different kinds of stupid for not "jumping on that". But I was too afraid.

Don't get me wrong. I wasn't popular. I was sexy. There's a difference. I lived in a poor neighborhood called the projects. It was a cruel awakening in comparison to the farm in Pennsylvania (talk about sudden culture shock) and a lot less safe! In the projects, every functional place (the mailboxes, wash house and the office) were in the center of the complex. My friends basically lived on my street. Otherwise, every other area screamed danger to me. So most of the time, I just stayed in like a hermit.

Fatherless and with a mother that was in school and working… we possessed very little in the way of material objects or stylish clothing. I was easily identified as different, shy and yes, dirty. For some reason, being poor has a ton of descriptions that are automatically assigned to you… for me it was nappy hair, dirty or shabby clothing, poor and for lack of a better word f***able. So, guys wanted to screw me (because I had a beautiful shape, pretty

27

eyes, a great smile and dimples) but not much more. Thank God I was smart enough to know that. I resolved within myself that I would never have sex.

One day my mom left a note for me to wash clothes. She was a full time student and worked a night job. So, if she left a note with a list of chores you'd better be sure to get them done or you would be in a lot of trouble when she got home.

Reluctantly, I headed over to the wash house. We lived upstairs from a woman that was an alcoholic and every now and again, you would hear her boyfriend beating her. She was standing in the doorway as I passed. She was a fairly heavy woman, older and beautiful but you could see the pain and drunkenness in her eyes. I crossed the street and walked the long sidewalk to the center of our complex.

In the wash house, there were two doors, one on each end of the small room. Washing machines lined one wall and dryers lined another. There was nowhere to sit and my mom REQUIRED I stay with the clothes when I washed them… otherwise someone could steal them.

So, I'd just finished washing a load or two when the boys showed up. There were 4 of them. Toothy grins and smart remarks began to fly as they followed each other on bicycles making loops through the wash room doors. They circled in and out of each door riding faster and faster. It scared the mess out of me. They kept making little sideways sexual statements saying they wanted me to do this and do that. I felt the fear inside of me begin to creep up my back. I was scared I was going to panic and run but I thought if I ran they would chase me. If they wanted to do something, what could I possibly of done to stop them?

In February of my freshman year this young man transferred in… he was from the north. He was a foot taller than me, wore a Chicago Bulls jacket and had a box with a nice fade haircut. His smile revealed perfect white teeth, soft lips and a faint hairline that suggested a mustache was growing in. He smelled amazing. I am not sure how but somehow, we became close friends. The relationship began with him and me just talking all the time. We would spend lunch together every day. We were discussing only God knows what, laughing… I don't even remember… all I remember is that we seemed to be kindred spirits.

One day my best friend (from church) asked if I and he wanted to hang out with and her and her boyfriend in the gym. It was colder that day so I said sure. (Ok, she was way more popular and I would have basically done anything she asked me to). While in the gym, he and I were laughing and having a good time (like always) when she suggested both groups go into the wrestling room. I probably should have known better… but I went without hesitation.

We went inside and sat down on the mats. It was completely dark because no one wanted to turn on the lights. He and I began kissing and groping and touching all kinds of body parts. I remember feeling his body change as he pressed against me. This was far different than my molester... up to this point, this boy and I had been no more than friends. We weren't writing love letters or anything. We were just friends I thought. But it was no doubt... I was madly in love with him from that day forward.

He and I were trying to think of all kinds of ways we could connect outside of school. It just so happened, he lived in the same apartments as one of my aunts. I would babysit her kids from time to time when she went to work. One evening, she was out and I called him. He begged me to come over his house and he didn't have to beg much. I was ready. I knew and he knew that it was possible I might be there and well, what can I say... we were waiting on this opportunity.

That evening I went to his apartment. When I walked in the first person I saw was his cousin who was in a higher grade. OH MY GOD. I had a mad crush on this guy from the first time I saw him at the bus stop one day. But, my love for Chicago was way stronger than my admiration for his cousin. His cousin commented, "Oh she's cute". This made me feel like the most beautiful girl in the world.

Sooner than later, he and I were in his room. We lay back on his bed and began kissing. I remember hearing DJ Quick's "Froggy Style" playing in the background. It didn't matter to me. All that mattered was that moment in time, in that space. Before you know it, it was over. I was pulling up my pants and sneaking back to my aunt's house.

As I headed back to her house, I was unsure how to process what was happening in my head or my heart as echoes of my virtuosity and virginity faded away.

Sophomore Year

My mother met a man… now I am not trying to say he was ugly, but he wasn't handsome either. He was an ex-convict that told her he'd dated Holly Robinson. Obviously, he knew how to pour on the charm. She talked like this guy was the best thing since sliced bread. He was about 6' 3", medium build and dark skinned. His face had all kinds of little moles on it and he had one of those weird mustaches. His eyes and smile were sinister and his whole atmosphere just reeked of sneakiness and up to no good. He talked like Flava Flav and looked like a cross between Flava Flav and Shaba from those music videos.

My mom graduated from college and soon our family moved to Tulsa and this guy moved in with us. I think that was a surprise because I don't remember my mom telling us that when we were moving... but, I guess she really didn't have to.

Between my mom working two jobs (at a daycare and Dillard's) to her boyfriend moving in with us, to the new neighborhood which was a step up but also a step back... Tulsa was a whirlwind! The high school reminded me of one of those high schools you see in movies about New York. I expected it to be named something nondescript like PS9...

The teachers really didn't care where you were, what you were doing and it was the most freedom I'd ever experienced in any school in my life. My popularity rating increased by 100 fold! The first week of school a senior carried me around on his shoulders to announce to the entire school I was his queen and my best friend was a senior girl that drove a Porsche. Her parents were loaded! I'd lost weight and well, Tulsa was looking up.

The coolest class I had was home economics. The teacher was a pot head for sure and came back every afternoon reeking of marijuana and extra high. It was 5th period and somehow I managed to stay in her class even in 6th period, always promising my physical science teacher (who asked me to join his swim team) a snicker doodle, cake or spaghetti to keep him from counting me absent. The boys in that class were cute and on a completely different level. I remember one boy asking me if I would come and sit on his face. I had no idea what he was talking about and everybody started laughing.

At the age of 15, and after losing my virginity, you would think my fear of men would have cascaded, but no it was raging ever more as adult men started to really hit on me and hard. This one guy, who was in his early 20's, really handsome, buff, dark skinned with gorgeous hazel eyes tried to date me over and over again. He came on to me really hard. He was a sweetheart and would never hurt me, but I was still scared of what a real relationship actually entailed. He was a Vice Lord gang member and banged real hard. All of the other guys he hung with in the gang were afraid of him. He was serious and deep in the gang activity but again was always so sweet to me. He was also a good friend of my brother.

One day my mom's boyfriend started a horrible fight with my mom. She broke his pinky finger as he tried to choke her by digging a set of keys into her throat. I remember walking in the house with a laundry basket on my hip and him yelling to me as soon as I got in. He was waving his pinky finger at me yelling, "See what your mama did, do you see what she did? She broke my pinky". I took one look at my mom and knew he deserved it. I was 15 at the time, and just the week before this man had beaten me so bad with a belt I had whelps that went from around my backside to the front of my belly button where the belt had wrapped around my body. (I deserved the butt whooping believe me but not to that degree). This guy was crazy.

When my mother wasn't home, we had a choice. Stay in or out. If we stayed in, he made my brother and I stay in our separate rooms, apart from each other as some sort of punishment. We would simply beat on the wall in a rhythmic pattern like rap stars to continue our commitment to spend time together. Once, we even opened both our bedroom windows and hung out of the windows to talk to each other and listen to the local radio station. But that didn't go well because a neighbor passing by knocked on the door and told on us (we were slightly on the roof).

On another occasion I sat on the steps of an apartment with my home girl across from our house. I was braiding her hair and we were laughing having fun… totally innocent. The next thing you know this crazy fool was on the porch yelling for my "hoe ass" to get in the house. Not only was I embarrassed, I was very upset. I wondered why my mother ever invited this man into our lives. He was obviously loony tunes.

Then she and he had another fight… a big one. My brother went to get his gang banging buddies and they came back in drones. Her boyfriend tried to leave in his itty bitty blue Toyota Corolla. As he was pulling out he yelled to the gang bangers that he would be back with his gun. That's when they dragged him out of the car and beat him like he stole something from their grandmother. That night my brother asked if his friends could stay the night. We all thought it was a good idea.

Just as suspected, around 2 am we hear rustling outside and the ramblings of a grown man that has had far too much to drink. He shattered the glass in the window downstairs in the front of our apartment in a poor attempt to break in. What he didn't know is that they were waiting for him. My brother delivered the first blow... a two by four bed slat to the arm as his hand crashed through the window. Within seconds the gang bangers were out the front door and beating him in front of our apartment.

All the while, my brother's best friend (who wasn't a gang banger) became homeless. With my mom's boyfriend gone it was much easier to sneak him into the house. He actually lived several months in my brother's closet.

My brother and I were close. He was my best friend and we shared many of the same friends. One night we went to an all-night neighborhood party/sleepover at our friend's house. We both lied to my mom about where we were going.

That night, before I got to tell my lie, my mom and I got into a horrible fight... I don't remember what it was about but I do remember calling my mom a bitch. She pulled me by my hair and lifted my feet off the ground. I remember thinking; oh that was a mistake… a big mistake.

I don't know how I talked her into letting me stay at my friend's house but she did. Now I think she probably thought that would be better than having me around.

My brother and I are about 11 months apart but you could have sworn we were twins the way we were connected. He has always protected me. Not trying to boast or anything, but we were beautiful to look at and had charismatic personalities. We were the life of the party at all parties!

Prior to this party, we were dating two people that decided they wanted to date each other on a weekend we left town to visit family. How adorable. This chick thought she was the bomb and my boyfriend must have thought that his booboo didn't stink because, they were bold with it. My brother and I laughed at them and knew revenge would be ours but the timing had to be right.

At the neighborhood party, it was time to execute our plan. My homeboy 'Hazel Eyes' was all over me all night. He couldn't stop talking to me and flirting with me. But he was a sweetheart so I welcomed it. Guys were offering me weed and everything else (when I started to smoke years later I'd wished I'd hit those joints but its best I didn't). The party was in one of the apartments.

Off hand, there were about 20-25 of us there. We were sitting on the floor, on the couch – wherever we could fit. Gang bangers, pot heads, car thieves, money making hoes, off brand chicks to name brand chicks, everyone was there. It was so much fun. Yes, we ran with a rough crowd, but growing up in the projects, you get used to the rough crowd. You don't even see what the world sees... you just see people, real people with real problems.

We were all sitting around drinking Strawberry Boones Farm and watching Scarface. 'Hazel Eyes' got super drunk (Lord knows what he was drinking) and began acting belligerent. I ignored him and began to flirt with the guy that started dating my brother's ex-girlfriend. It was time for revenge.

The next thing you know he was holding my hand coercing me into the bathroom. It was hilarious. I could see my brothers off brand ex-girlfriend getting all excited as she watched us. They were supposed to still be dating! That's when my brother went and started talking to her best friend. In the bathroom my brother's best friend and I started kissing. He tried to take it further, fumbling around my bra hooks and what not when I stopped him. I looked him in the eye and yelled, "You left me and played me and my brother for that off brand chick? After we let your homeless ass live in our house for months? Don't you ever in your life talk to me again." I thought I was hard, and truth be told, I was. I didn't like anybody trying to play me like some type of idiot or even worse, hurting my brother. My brother was too good to this chump. I got up and walked out feeling like I was queen bee. His faced dropped as I headed outside to see what 'Hazel Eyes' was up to.

My homeboy was sick y'all. 'Hazel Eyes' was spinning around in circles with a gun in his hand in the middle of the courtyard. He was screaming that he was the greatest. He was totally out of control. His head was stuck in some Scarface mess. I went back in the house to kick it with my home girls.

Really, we had a great group of friends in Tulsa. We were tight and made memories I won't soon forget. From the girls I got arrested with for shoplifting at the local gas station to one of those crazy adult guys pulling down his pants to reveal a penis that dropped down to his knees during a game of hide and go get it… to being stuck in the theater watching Class Act because a tornado threatened to hit the mall… we had great times! We shared moments of pain, shock, disappointment, embarrassment but most of all fun. We were poor, living in the projects having a great time cheering as echoes of our ignorance and benevolent obedience to all things righteous faded before our eyes.

Junior Year

Then we moved to Oklahoma City. My mom got a job as a teacher in an all-black middle school. They were in an independent school district but of course, we were enrolled in the all-white high school across town, to keep us out of trouble…

The only black kids that attended that school lived in our neighborhood which was certainly the projects. When my mom finished college, she chased opportunity and if it meant moving that is what we did.

My brother wasn't in a gang but he traveled heavily with the gang members. He knew every member well and could do the gang signs and walk the walk. He banged just as hard as they did but he never became a member and never got in any trouble.

The best thing about moving to OKC was my friendship with my cousin. Mainly because I began smoking weed and my cousin had "the connect". He didn't hesitate to bring me a joint or two when he would come by. We were also really good friends. We would laugh and talk all the time. Our conversations would last for hours. We talked about school, Tupac and Jesus. He would tell me about his adventures and I would tell him about mine. The girls I went to school with knew him and were madly in love with him and fighting over him all the time. I fought for him and he fought for me. We were both in the same gang and everything. It may sound crazy, but it was really a blessing. I needed his friendship.

During that summer, my mom went on a work trip to California. She left the car keys. Since middle school I'd snuck and drove the car around the block every time my mom would ask me to start it in the morning… and I'd finally taught myself how to drive. So, one night while she was out of town, I took a bunch of my home girls to the local teen club. We had so much fun! We danced and laughed and saw all of our friends from high school. When we got home, one of my home girls' boyfriend and his friends were sitting outside the apartment and we all began to drink beer.

It was a great summer night. You could see the stars in the sky and the colors of the sky, trees, grass and shine from the different color cars beneath the parking lot lights just seemed to shine brightly.

As we are all outside enjoying ourselves a guy from school that belonged to a rival gang (of her boyfriends) started walking through our neighborhood. *He didn't belong in our complex.* He lived up the street. I know at one point in time he tried to date one of my home girls and he and she were arguing. They'd gotten into it at school a couple of times but it never resulted in much. Well, they were arguing again.

The next thing you know, he pulled out a gun. Now, I'd seen guns. I've had guys put loaded guns in my lap as they run into grocery stores and clean their guns in front of me. I'd seen them shoot them during holidays in celebration… But, I never saw anyone pull a gun out and aim it before… not with real intent!

When he pulled that gun out, he pointed it directly at the girl that was arguing with him. My friend and her sister was 8-months pregnant and standing right beside her. Her boyfriend screamed for her to run as he ran to protect his girlfriend. He ran directly in front of her.

I guess the commotion scared the boy with the gun because that's when you heard the shots. The baby's father fell to the ground instantly and a pool of blood began to pour from his body.

There were about 8 of us. We chased the boy with the gun until he reached the fence and jumped over. I lost both of my flip-flops in the chase. My toes were caked with mud as I finally ran back to sit with my home girl. She sat crying, her bulging belly awkwardly weighing her down as she rocked holding his hand.

I prayed for God to heal him. I promised her it would be ok. I prayed fervently. God always answered my prayers. But… he didn't that night. I watched this young man I'd only recently became friends with die. I held his other hand as it became cold and I watched his eyes roll in the back of his head. *I couldn't believe he was dead.*

The police left his dead body on the ground until late into the morning. When the medical examiner finally arrived around 4 am, they made us all go and give statements at the police station… they wouldn't even let me get a pair of shoes. I sat in the cold police office with muddy feet for more than 6 hours.

When we returned home at about 10 am, he was still lying there on the ground. There wasn't even a sheet on his body. It was surreal. *In those moments, echoes of lost life, angry words and uneasiness panged back in forth in my mind as I wondered why God didn't answer my prayer.*

Senior Year

Somewhere between Tulsa and Oklahoma City, my brother and sister and I went to visit my dad in Atlanta with his new wife also known as the woman that stole him from my mom. We didn't get along and two weeks into a "summer" long vacation, I'd called my grandpa to come back and get us.

My grandpa promised me when he dropped us off that if we didn't want to stay he would come get us and he did just what he promised. At the time, my dad, his wife and our two new little brothers lived in an apartment in Stone Mountain. Georgia red clay and walking to the gas station for Heath bars were the acme of excitement. I lived for candy bar wrappers with discount coupons or another free Heath bar inside. It was pretty boring to say the least. I hated it. My dad is a very spiritual man and he would always be in the back room praying or reading his bible.

Movies and television watching were our best times. My dad is super funny. He can break down a scenario very quickly and in the most humorous of manners. I remember one day we were watching Oprah and Stevie Wonder was a guest on the show. My dad started laughing and cocked his head to the side, then said "Awww man, why they got Stevie on here looking like the predator? Somebody should have told him. They got him jacked up." We'd just watched the Predator on laser disc (technology is my dad's other big thing besides God) and his comments rendered an hour of laughter for me. It wasn't just the content, it was the delivery. For a man that seemed so serious about so much it was always good to laugh with him.

My dad rarely worked. I am sure I irritated his wife to death with my sideways comments and overt dislike for the situation as a whole. At one point and time the older of my new little brothers got sick and they had to call the ambulance. They had to pump his stomach. He'd swallowed several aspirin.

Now it was senior year and my father was visiting for my graduation. *Woop tee doo.* My mom was mad, my dad was disappointed and I was angry. My brother and sister seemed to be happy he was there but I just couldn't be.

I was barely graduating. Earlier in the year I had been on punishment from September to Thanksgiving for smoking weed on our patio with my friends. My punishment? I couldn't walk to the pay phone at the local gas station to talk to my friends who knew the number and called me on a regular basis. I'd also dated a guy who was a serious gangbanger. I didn't know he already had a girlfriend and when he brought me two handfuls of rings to wear that he'd taken them directly from her. He let me drive his 1982 Cutlass Supreme a couple of times and once when we went to the mall we were shot at. I eventually broke up with him because he was a habitual liar, but later I learned that he was killed… or it was suicide… I am still not sure. He had a lot of enemies. At any rate, I was full of anger, rage and some other stuff. I am not sure why I was so mad… I just was.

I paid my dad no mind. I went and hung out with my friends and acted like he wasn't even there. I didn't like him at all. In fact, I hated him. I resented him for not being there… for not caring. So what he came for graduation… that is what he was supposed to do.

I can still feel the vibration of my father's footsteps as he walked away, I imagine deciding to never visit us or Oklahoma again.

Chapter 4

All it Takes is One Step to Go on a Thousand Mile Journey

That summer I met the most beautiful man I have ever seen. Well, maybe not the most beautiful but pretty damn close. He was tall and light skinned with a gorgeous smile. He carried himself in a way that was simply adorable. You can say it was love at first sight… all I can say is it had to be destiny.

We met at Penn Square Mall. I was waiting on my cousin to order her Taco Bell in the food court and he was coming up the escalator. It was a bad hair day! I almost didn't make it to the mall! But, my cousin was visiting for the summer and she insisted. The only reason I agreed is because I had on my favorite deep purple Cross Colour shorts that were cut extra short and made my butt look huge. As a thick girl with a great top and bottom, pretty eyes and a great smile… I knew my hair couldn't block what I had going on. My cousin and I were standing in line waiting for her to order when this guy walks up to us and offers me his number. He was handsome but not nearly as adorable as the guy on the escalator. After getting his telephone number I saw the guy I'd locked eyes with from the escalator standing near the Wendy's with his friends. There was a hallway entrance to the restrooms right next to him. I walked past him making sure NOT to look at him. A couple of minutes later, when I came out, he was standing right next to that hall as if he was waiting on me. He said, "Excuse me, but can we be friends?"

It was the right thing to say to me. I had recently been in a couple of tumultuous relationships and right out of high school. I wasn't looking for a relationship. In fact, I'd been dating this guy that was way older than me and had 3 kids and it was NOT working out.

The next day, he and I talked for hours. I remember smoking a whole pack of Newports as I sat at the payphone in my apartments and talked to him. I remember him telling me that I was the type of woman he could marry. I laughed it off and dismissed it as we kept talking. By 18, I thought I knew the game better than men. Men were always selling wolf tickets… trying to tell you whatever it was they thought you wanted to hear… just so they could hit it.

The next day, he came to pick me up. I had him stop by my current boyfriend's house. I remember walking in and saying hey to his homeboys, going back to his bedroom and letting him know… it was over. He didn't argue, he just said, "Ok" and I left. My new man and I were together ever since.

We dated all summer. Going to the arcade, going to the movies, going to the mall… we went everywhere together and we were together every day. I met several of his friends and he met mine.

That summer I also enrolled in college. It was a city college and not the university… where I wanted to go. I was disappointed that I couldn't afford to go the university. Campus life was just a dream.

But community college was cool because I loved the classes and the students. I met a lot of people that felt like I did... freshman that wished they were going to the university too... yet grateful to be in school.

At any rate, I liked the classes but I loved my boyfriend more. I ended up dropping out of college and moving in with him. By May, I was pregnant. The day I found out, I begged him to go to Sonic Drive-In to get me something to eat. When he came back, I was throwing up in the toilet. He took one look at me and said, "You're pregnant!" I said, "No way". He said, "Yes you are."

I don't know if he was trying to get me pregnant or what... but I was and there was nothing I could do about it. He already had an older daughter. She was born a week or so after I met him. She was beautiful. But, that didn't mean that I was ready to have a baby. I remember calling my mom and telling her. She insisted I go to the doctor to verify and I did.

I was nauseas the entire pregnancy. It was so bad, anything I smelt would turn my stomach. It was cold too. It sucked being pregnant.

On December 28, 1999, I gave birth to my oldest daughter. I was amazed at how beautiful and obviously intelligent she was. She had a head full of hair, pretty brown eyes and light skin.

By the time our daughter was two months old, he and I were

married. We married at the church I spent my latter childhood in, in Muskogee. My pastor married us. As we prepared for our modest wedding, it was decided I should go up ahead of time. I was to get my hair done and make sure all the preparations at the church were ready. Really, if it wasn't for my aunt... I don't think it would have happened. She steer headed it all. My grandmother bought my wedding dress and his mom bought his suit.

I have a lot of family and they were all there to celebrate. In the salon, one of my cousins asked, "So he asked you to marry him, and you are here but he is not? What if he doesn't show up?" I thought about her question and said, "No he is going to be here, I know it."

It was nice to have so much family support. I remember my Aunt teasing us when we'd visited for Thanksgiving the year before... "You two just gonna play house? You better marry my niece." Yup, I blame her for us getting married to this day. He always tried to prove to everyone that he loved me. He was an only child so he loved being in a big family. In some ways, he'd grown close to my brother and my cousins. It was the beginning of great memories.

Right before the wedding started, I remember telling my grandmother that I was nervous. My stomach hurt so bad I felt like there were huge knots in it. She told me, "It's because you have butterflies. It's ok to be nervous. This is an important decision." It was. I was only 19 and I knew I had my whole life ahead of me. I remember at one point having aspirations to be a lawyer… but God almost instantly told me no. I still remember where I was standing and what I was thinking. It was on a day my dad was supposed to call me. I was again waiting by one of those payphones in the apartments. It began to rain but I was determined to wait… I didn't want to miss his call. I'd been thinking about becoming a criminal defense attorney because of people like Nancy Grace that thought they knew everything. She was hot headed and full of hot air… or so I thought (now I am one of the biggest Nancy Grace fans). At any rate, God dismissed that idea as fast as it had entered. That day in the rain was when I decided that the only father I needed was God. I knew I could depend on him to see me through any and all situations. Almost the next day, I met my boyfriend. Now, here I was ready to walk down the aisle with him.

My dad didn't come to my wedding. Maybe he had something more important to do, all I know is I called and invited him and the day of (after the wedding) he called to tell me he wasn't going to make it. Instead, my mom's brother walked me down the aisle. It was beautiful. I was super nervous too. I giggled through the entire ceremony. I mean the ENTIRE ceremony. I was just so nervous!

I couldn't have imagined two years ago as a gangbanging high school student that I would be getting married at 19! But, I was and I did.

I hate big crowds, big parties and crowded places. I also hated being asked weird personal questions about our future and how happy we were together. My family planned a really nice reception at my grandmother and grandfather's house but I insisted we duck out early and go straight to the honeymoon. I just wanted to spend time with my new husband... especially now that we had a babysitter. Our honeymoon was in Tulsa. We couldn't afford more but it was nice. He drove us to our hotel. We finally relaxed. Life had been throwing us curveballs and we finally felt like we were ahead of the game. We were just happy to be. We enjoyed each other immensely as we basked in our new found level of commitment.

Pregnant Again...

A year hadn't passed and I was pregnant again. I couldn't believe it. I was working at a pizza shop and my life already wasn't what I'd hoped it would be. Our newborn was a lot for me then and despite my husband working all day and night... we were broke and I couldn't imagine what would come next. We did not believe we could afford to financially or emotionally care for another child. We decided an abortion would be best. No one would have to know and life could go on as it currently was.

One block away from the clinic, my husband stopped the car.

51

I was crying uncontrollably about the horrible act I was about to commit. I was scared out of my mind and so sad that this was the choice I "wanted" to make. He firmly said to me, "We don't have to do this. We can take care of this child."

I wish I could tell you I made the "right" choice. But I can't.

We drove to the clinic and I had the abortion. I say I, because the moment my husband gave me a choice, it became my decision. I've had to OWN that decision ever since.

Each year as Mother's Day rolls around I find myself wondering about my "son".

The abortion took a major toll on me. I was depressed for about 2 ½ years. I wouldn't allow my husband to touch me and I couldn't stand anything related to sex. It was a hard time. I remember having this feeling in the back of my head that because I wasn't having sex with him, my husband was always cheating on me.

At first, it was nothing to me. I would compensate by flirting with the cutest guy in a room long enough to make him think we were going home together. I began to go to the club on the weekends with my best friend from high school. She was gorgeous and after my first child, I dropped so much weight… I was too!

In the parking lot before entering the club she and I would get "lifted". She would drink and I would smoke weed. We didn't want to have to buy any drinks once we got inside. Then we'd find some guys to buy drinks for us.

Hitting the Streets

I had a beautiful caramel colored Cutlass Supreme, a newer model with the curved body. I thought I was the stuff in that car. I was beautiful with a gorgeous body… who could tell me different? The front license plate read, "Brown Sugar"… my older cousin had it made for me. So one night, I drove my best friend to the club and by the time we got there we were so drunk and high we hadn't realized I'd parked smack dab in the middle of a mud ditch. It wasn't so bad and I was able to strategically get out of the car. There wasn't anywhere else to park. You could hear the melodic beats thumping loudly from the club as we walked in, with the chants of those inside as each part of the song directed them to respond. The club was poppin'.

We had one of the best times ever that night! By the time we got done partying, staggering to the car, numbers from sexy guys safely tucked into our pockets… we walked out to find the front two tires completely immersed in mud with no help in sight. Out of all those guys that wanted to take us home none of them were willing to help us. Even security had an attitude! They had to call a tow truck to pull us out the ditch. It was like 6 am when we finally got home.

Cheating didn't come easy but it eventually roared its head. I always felt better than that. I didn't mind if someone thought I was cheating… as long as I never crossed that line. But, the greater the distance between my husband and I, the more I craved for someone to love me.

It started with meeting a guy and kissing/groping after the club. Whispering empty promises in his ear knowing I would never fulfill them. Then it turned into calling the guy… meeting him, having sex in odd places at odd times. I never had a problem lying to my husband because somewhere in the back of my mind, I always knew he was lying to me…. I just needed someone to validate my existence and appreciate my presence. I literally remember writing in a journal to God that I needed to get some dick. I actually wrote that --- to God! Looking back on all those old journal entries makes me laugh, but it is so telling about my state of mind!

My oldest daughter was innocent and beautiful, a witness to all the darkness that lied between us and a light in our lives that couldn't help but shine. She was my bestie. We watched movies together, went shopping together and had tons of fun. Even though I worked two jobs most of my life, I still found time for her.

Almost four years after our first daughter was born, we were still going strong. Weathering our storms with what small semblance of love was left. The cheating had stopped and we were rebuilding.

Soon, we were pregnant with our second daughter – a true

blessing from God. My second pregnancy was tough… my second daughter was a feisty one. She kicked and moved around so much! I remember hoping and praying she was a boy. When the doctor told me she was a girl, I cried and cried. I was depressed for two days. I remember telling myself, I killed my son. I felt worthless as a woman.

But when my baby was born, she was gorgeous. She was dark skinned with pretty dimples and eyes that sparkled. Her personality was so strong we knew she was going to have a demanding and prominent voice wherever she went. Her older sister loved on her from the day she was born.

Our family was beautiful and from the outside looking in, you would never imagine what went on behind our closed doors. No one could or would as long as I could help it. I wanted our private lives to be private… and I guess I still do. I think it is so important to respect the privacy of others… because I would want someone to do the same for me.

I was beautiful. I knew it because people told me all the time. But it didn't matter how pretty I was on the outside, I couldn't change what was on the inside. Inside I was still that molested little girl that grew up in the projects. I was still that little girl her daddy didn't want. The one that never knew what life with a real man was supposed to be like.

My insecurities eventually pushed me to do what my mind and heart never felt were a good idea… I stayed married to my husband. Truth is, I loved him and probably always will as he was my first love. But, I can't say it was the smartest choice.

I feel like this is a good place to stop talking about my marriage. Just know that many events transpired that caused me to look at myself and my marriage in a different way.

Time to Grow

I worked at a car rental company as a reservation agent. Work and home life were black and white. I was always a good employee. I knew our systems backward and forward. Once, one of my uncles told me how to move up in the company was to always go for those new open positions. That's exactly what I did. If there was an opportunity that paid more and required more learning, I went for it. After going as far as I could in one department, I went on to another. Eventually, I was promoted to the Alpha department. It was about $1 and some change more an hour and a more relaxing shift, even if it was graveyard.

I love to draw and write. I would make posters and desktop art for my coworkers all of the time. I remember once a friend was reading this romantic book and she detailed a scene she loved to me. The next morning when she came in, I'd drawn the scene on her desktop. She laughed and enjoyed it. One of my coworkers, a close friend, told me I should become a graphic designer. At first I laughed, but when I thought it through, I thought... it would be really cool. I decided to go for it.

To go to technology school, they require you take entrance exams. So, the day arrived that I was to go and take my TABE (Test of Adult Basic Education) test. The test was scheduled for 8 am. I got off of work at 7:30 am and planned to head straight to the school. I went out after my graveyard shift and my car wouldn't start. I was distraught and a bit overwhelmed with grief. Then my coworker and friend that convinced me to go to school's shift had ended and she came out to see me standing next to my car. She saw the look of disappointment on my face. She insisted I get in the car with her. I shook my head, "no". I remember her uttering an "uh-uh" and looking me square in the eye. She dropped me off at the school and I aced the test. I remember the admittance counselor telling me almost no one scores perfect on that test... but I did. That woman changed my life with one act of kindness!

I immediately started class. I would work my graveyard shift from 11:30 pm to 7:30 am and go directly to school from 8 am to 12 pm. Within a year, I became a part time artist in the marketing department at the school while still working graveyard at Hertz. I would work in marketing from 12 pm – 3pm. After 2 years in school, I learned enough about animation design with the part time work for the video producer in marketing to create a demo reel. The reel got me hired at one of the best television stations in our market. I worked there most days from 4 to 10 pm. Yes, you can do the math. I worked 7 days a week, and most days I worked anywhere from 14 – 20 hours. This went on for about 6 months… I was hitting year 5 at rental company (fully vested 401K) and I was holding out for that day.

During my career development, things were getting worse at home. I was a praying woman… not that I believed they went past the ceiling but talking to God was an everyday thing for me.

My husband's oldest daughter was nine. She'd been living with her grandmother who'd just passed away. Her mother was pregnant and insisted that my husband take care of her. He brought her home and that was that. No questions, no answers, just take care of my child. She was a beautiful creative and outgoing girl. She looked exactly like my husband with big beautiful eyes and the same face. She lived with us for about a year and a half.

After working at the news station for about 2 years, I was offered a full-time job at the technology center. Salary, benefits, and an office… a dream come true. I couldn't believe it! I was finally down to one good job. That's also when I decided that after 9 years of marriage we should get a divorce.

My daughters and I left and moved into our own apartment…

I can still hear the echoes and pitter patter of little feet as we walked away from our only chance at having a complete family.

Chapter 5

In the Silence Hearts Break... But in the Noise There is Trouble

Right after I left my husband, I was sent on a business trip to Chicago. I was attending the HOW Design Conference, it was made for designers and creative of every walk. I was like a kid in a candy store. They had so many offerings to choose from it was hard to select between this class or the next. The hotel I stayed in was shabby sheik at best, but I was late registering and they had a million conferences in Chicago that week. I was good to get a room! The conference began with a party opener. I'd gone online prior to leaving for Chicago to find out more about the conference. They had a meet and greet area for conference attendees to network and meet others that would go. I connected a group of people that promised to meet for drinks the first night of the conference. The group I met included one African American guy, one Caucasian guy, one Caucasian female and an Asian guy. They were a lot of fun and flew in from California, Georgia and Texas. We had drinks and promised to connect the next day. It was good to know somebody at the conference!

We met up the next day during break and had lunch. Two of the guys in the group worked in Atlanta at a national magazine. They were a lot of fun to hang out with. They told crazy stories about their staff and creative workflow back in Atlanta.

Everywhere you went in the conference, some vendor was giving you a sample of something. Whether it was paper, t-shirts, point of purchase merchandise or a jump drive with their presentations slapped on them, you ended up walking away with another suitcase of promotional items. Two days in, I realized there was no way I was getting all of this stuff into my luggage.

The FedEx desk at the conference hotel was backed up. The line wasn't too long but there was a wait. I moved along the assembly line they prepared for conference goers and finally arrived at my last stop. What stood before me was a 6 foot dark chocolate man with the most beautiful eyes and sexiest voice. He was exquisite to look at. His eyes were hypnotic. His hair was smooth with tight curls and his lips were beautiful and deliciously tempting. He had a way about him that just intrigued me. (smile)

We hammered out the final details needed to ship my package and he assured me that all of my materials would arrive safely. I turned to walk away feeling very pleasant because that was a nice encounter. Who knew so much attraction could be had simply creating a Pack and Ship order? Just as I began to walk away he said, "Ms. Moore". I turned around and he motioned for me to come forward. He looked me in the eye and firmly said, "Do you mind if I call you later?"

I was still married… but it was no secret our marriage was ending. I'd given my husband a year from the day I moved out to get it together or we would be divorced. So, I gave the beautiful man standing before me my telephone number. He smiled and told me he would be sure to call me. And… that would have been great IF I hadn't left my cell phone in the taxi cab between conference and dinner (look at God). Knowing me, if I was able to meet him for drinks that evening, I probably would have left Chicago pregnant. But, I lost my cell phone and couldn't be reached until I'd secured a new phone in Oklahoma two days later. When I finally secured a new phone from US Cellular it was a day or two before I got a call one night from a Chicago area code.

One of the first things he said to me was, "I have to tell you something. However you decide to receive it is totally up to you". I said "ok" and waited to hear what he had to say. He explained that he was married but separated from his wife. He told me about his son he fathered at the age of 15 and his adopted children in marriage. He told me about his grandmother who was his closest friend. He told me about his mother and his baby sister who he adored so much. That evening he bared his soul to me, without knowing me. He squarely explained he understood if he had or carried too much for me to manage or accept.

His confession relieved me. It allowed me to confess that I too was married and separated. I explained some of the drama that I'd recently gone through, the shame, the hurt and the pain. That night we talked until we fell asleep on the phone together. Our conversation was about 7 hours long.

This man and I fast became best friends. His words made love to my mind and restored the self-reflection of beauty for my internal being that seemingly had vanished. His presence made me feel whole and complete. I felt like he was an angel sent to save me at one of my deepest moments of despair, anguish and loneliness.

Despite our distance, we spent 18 of 24 hours on the phone talking to each other each day. He allowed me to transcend the mileage that separated us and invited me into a place most men keep off limits... his mind. We spoke all day, and I felt as though I went everywhere he went. Whether that was a train or a house party, work or over his grandmothers... I was right there with him. Talking to his friends and laughing at things they said. He would explain to me what I couldn't see through his eloquent use of words.

He was a security guard so I talked to him a majority of his shifts. I knew I was falling in love with him. The first time he told me he wanted to kiss me, or hold me, my heart skipped a beat and my stomach felt funny. I knew I wanted him to hold me more than he could have ever wanted to hold me. I desired this man that made my mind race with wonder... that filled my mind with peace, that reassured my inner beauty was real and not fictitious. I wanted this man to hold me and never let me go.

65

We laughed, whispered, I cried, we moaned. We were one in more ways than I could describe. The one thing that made him stand out more than any other man I would meet, was his innate sense of self. He knew himself and why he made every choice he's ever made. His memory recall was way better than mine and his study of life in general was all-inclusive and never excluded a specific type of person for any reason. No doubt, I loved this man for his mind and his soul and most of all, for his heart.

He and I watched a ton of movies together. We would rent the same movie just so we could watch it. He had his version on and I had mine on and we did our best to synchronize the timing of the voices. We both created video tapes to send one another and we would email each other funny things we found online or photos. He was my man and I was his woman. There was no question in my mind he loved me as much as I loved him.

We had to see each other. Our phone romance had to become something real and tangible. He rode the bus for 24 hours from Chicago to Oklahoma City. We talked the entire ride as he described passengers and locations he was in. The closer he got, the more excited I got. Then, the moment arrived. He was here. I couldn't believe he was actually here.

My heart pounded out of control as I pulled into the Greyhound bus station. There were a lot of men standing around outside and it was chilly. We'd met in June and here it was a couple of months later and he was actually coming back to my house with me.

I wore a yellow jacket with a white stripe down the arms. I wore a white mini-skirt to match. I made sure my makeup and hair were beautiful... but I was still nervous. As soon as I saw him, I nervously walked up to him. I stood right in front of him and looked up into his beautiful eyes. He looked down at me and wrapped his arms around me. He hugged me tight. To this day, it remains the best hug I have ever had in my life.

If I could imagine what a hug from God would feel like I think it would be just like that hug was: safe, warm and loving. But of course, God's would be better because he's God! But, that is how I felt and that is really how I still feel.

On the ride home, all I could do was tie his image before me to the voice I'd grown to love. My kids were over at my mom's house. When we arrived to my house, we kissed for a long time and then he went to take a shower. Afterwards, we talked and kissed, then made love. Looking him in the eye and telling him that I loved him as we climaxed was one of the best feelings. He was physically and mentally all I would ever need in a man. Money has never been a big attracter for me. I love words and touch... and this man knew how to do both well.

He came to visit me a couple of times. I went to visit him a couple of times. Sometimes he flew, sometimes I drove. One time he came to visit and one of my uncles fell sick. It was bad. My family called and asked all family members to head to Muskogee (about 2 and ½ hours from home). We are a praying family and we believe in the healing power of Jesus. So, we were all called to come down and pray. I wanted for him to come with me but he refused. He was tired and had already been on a long trip coming to see me. This was going to be his longest visit and he'd just arrived.

He opted not to go and I was angry. We began to argue. It was horrible. I would say memories of bad days in my past and his past interfered with our present argument… and it didn't end well. I was so angry I told him that he could go home and dropped him off at the bus station. I knew he didn't have any more money because he'd spent it all coming to see me. And I ignorantly assumed he would still be there when I got back… but he was gone. He'd snuck on a bus and had a friend send money to help him get home. I was heartbroken. This was the trip we decided would measure if we could make it work together on a longer term basis. We failed and it hurt.

We broke up. It was hard for me. I had grown to love this man with all that was in me. I'd never felt this way before. Even in my marriage, I guess because my husband never captured my mind the way he did. When what we had ended, I truly felt like I had lost a part of me.

I hated myself and wanted so badly to cover my pain with new love, new admiration, new anything that would help to take my mind off of him.

Desperate, Destitute and Depraved

I started talking to this guy on BlackPlanet.com. At the time, I loved the website. It was the closest semblance to Facebook and connected me with black people everywhere. I loved it. It was great to see what people in other markets found interesting or worth sharing.

That's when and how I met this guy named "Green eyes"... at least that is what his profile said... I know you are thinking... what was his real name? I found out and he told me but at the end of the day, that's all I really remember.

Anyway, this guy told me he was coming to Oklahoma on business and would love to meet me. I wanted to get my mind off my recent heartbreak and decided it was a good idea. He was from New Jersey.

When he came to pick me up for our date, I had him meet me at my mother's house. She was babysitting my daughters. He met my mom and we went out. I wish I had her write his tag number down.

He was very courteous, tall and handsome and yes... he had

green eyes. So, he and I went to dinner then went back to my house. He'd purchased champagne and orange juice to make mimosas... which I thought was great because it was my first mimosa. I remember we were watching JoJo Dancer. He pulled out his weed and began to roll a blunt. At any rate, we didn't get far into the movie before I was extremely tired. I hadn't drank that much... I mean I only had one drink and nothing to drink at dinner. It was crazy for me to be so tired. I mean unusually tired.

I told him I was going to lie down. I went into my bedroom. When I woke up he was asking me to take my pants off. I told him I didn't want to, that I wasn't ready for anything like that. He began taking my pants off anyway. They were white pants. I can still see the pants leg coming down off of my legs. I was too tired to fight and I drifted off back to sleep. The next time I woke up, I could feel him inside of me. He was lying behind me on the bed and he had his arm around my neck, I was in the headlock. One of my arms was pinned beneath me and the other was pulled back next to him. I remember crying and telling him he didn't have to do this. I would just give it to him if he stopped. I felt a tear run down my cheek. He began to choke me until I passed out again.

When I woke up I felt this crazy stickiness between my legs. It was blood. I got up and went to my bathroom. When I came out I saw him wrapped up in my blanket like a cocoon. He was bold and obviously didn't know how crazy I am. I was still a little groggy but cognizant enough to kill him if I so desired. I remember going to get the switchblade I kept on a shelf in my closet. It was my father-in-laws that I took from my husband before I left. I had it for times just like these…

I contemplated cutting his throat… several times. I wanted to wake him up with blood between his legs. But, I kept thinking about what my kids would think. What they would have to face. No matter how I ran the headline in my head… they would know. Everyone would know I invited some strange man into my home and I got what I deserved. I couldn't tell anyone. Eventually, he woke up and left.

The only person I knew I could tell was the man I'd fallen in love with. I called him and apologized to him. We hadn't spoken in a while. He was angry and I was angry so we just stayed away from each other for a while. I called him sobbing. He was the only person I felt like I could trust with the information without being judged. I was right. He understood why I did what I did and he better explained to me why I couldn't blame myself, even though everything in me said otherwise.

He was sorry about what happened to me. I couldn't go to work… I took the day off and talked to him for maybe 30 minutes short of 24 hours. This was the day I realized I would love him

71

for the rest of my life… no matter what. He didn't judge me. He understood and felt really bad about what happened. At the time, neither of us had any money. This was a day and time before unlimited calling and text (remember those days?) and we often ate our budgets with high phone bills trying to stay connected.

I called my sister and begged her to buy a ticket for him to come and see me online. And she did it. But wait, you don't understand how BIG this is. If you knew my sister this is something I never would have expected her to do. Nor would I have even asked. But, maybe she heard something in my voice. Maybe, she knew somehow… I don't know. She's a compassionate person and she loves me… so maybe that's why she did it. She also knew I was in love with him… and maybe that's why. I don't know… maybe it was just ordained by God.

Within 2 days of my rape, he flew in and was in my house comforting me. I was so thankful for his friendship. I remember having a doctor's appointment to check for STD's and HIV for the next morning. But, I just wanted to be held. I just wanted him to hold me and not let me go. I wanted to feel safe. I loved him so much. This was the first time my kids met him. I couldn't tell my mom about the rape, because I was ashamed. So, my kids didn't have anywhere else to go, so they met him then.

They all got along really well. He loved my kids as an extension of me. He took the time to connect with them on their level. I would never invite a man into my house while my kids were home. I am really strong about that… but in this instance… I needed him to be there for me to feel safe. So we all sat and watched "That's So Raven" together… which really comforted me to no end.

After I put the kids in the bed, he and I began to talk. He told me how important it was to make sure I was safe. That he understood that I wanted to date and that was healthy but my safety and my children's safety were more important than giving into my emotions. He counseled me all night from a "friend's" position. I thanked him and we hugged each other all night long.

In the middle of the night, we began to kiss and one thing led to another. We ended up having sex. At one point during sex I looked down to see he was having sex with me through his boxers. He didn't have any condoms and he didn't want to offend me but I had just been raped… it crushed me all over again. I understood… but it still hurt. I wanted this seemingly long stream of never ending pain and rejection to end.

The next morning at the doctor's office, I felt like a slut. The white older doctor treated me like everything was my fault. When he examined me, he knew I'd had sex recently… He asked me about my rape again and repeated it all… He just looked at me like I was the biggest idiot in the world. Truth be told, looking back it was

73

stupid. But, I can't say I wouldn't do it again because sex was the only consistent thing in my life. I remember one day my friend emphasized it to me, "Stephanie, sex is NOT love". But it served as validation of my worth in my eyes. The doctor promised to send me my test results. And they came back all negative… I was relieved.

I wanted him to move to Oklahoma but since the bus thing… he wasn't coming. The last time he visited, he'd actually already almost secured a job in Oklahoma and I had no idea until later… after the rape. Evidently, he'd experienced some racist remarks and attitudes while here and he told me he could never move to Oklahoma.

In the meanwhile, the rapist kept calling me. He would tell me he loved me. He called me baby. He wanted to see me. I was scared out of my mind. I never reported it because I just didn't have the nerve to tell anyone what happened and I didn't want my daughters to find out. I changed my number. But he got my new number. He kept saying he loved me. It was freaky and frightening.

My sister recently moved to Atlanta, my brother and father were in Atlanta… it was time to move. I knew it was what God wanted me to do from the beginning. I loved my new job and my nice office. I didn't want to leave but I was scared the rapist would show up at my house one day and I wouldn't know what to do. I also didn't want to be the only one of my siblings stuck in Oklahoma while my little sister and brother chased their dreams.

As I packed to leave Oklahoma and head to Atlanta, echoes of love lost and new pain resounded in my heart.

Chapter 6

Nine Lives... and Then Some

I asked my brother and cousin to help me move. My small apartment was upstairs in a shabby complex near my job. The apartment was about 1100 sq. ft. and full of junk my daughters and I had accumulated over the years. We are something like hoarders! I knew it was moving day and as I looked around my house I realized, I hadn't packed a single thing. At least I had boxes!

When my brother arrived, he was so angry at me that he punched a hole in my wall. This made me angry. He knew I didn't have the money to pay for that and that it would ruin my ability to get my deposit back. That made me angry.

I'd rented a 14-foot truck and we'd filled it to capacity. I had one additional bag of my favorite shoes. It contained beautiful heels in a plethora of different colors and styles. He went over and threw it in the dumpster. My favorite shoes were in that bag! He was flipping out. It was partially my fault (I could have certainly done a better job) but for the most part he was on ten for no reason.

When we finally finished packing we went to my mother's house. My nerves were on edge, we had a long trip ahead of us, everyone was angry and my mom. She got the worst of it. I can't even remember what she said, all I remember is being extremely angry and cussing her out. I'd never spoken so many cuss words at one time and in my heart I knew I was wrong. I had a lot of anguish pent up inside and anger toward my mom. There was a more graceful way to express what I felt, but I didn't choose that route. I was really ready to get to Atlanta and leave all the mess Oklahoma represented behind me. Little did I know, I would only be taking the mess with me because it wasn't represented in a place at all.

My brother, who loves me dearly but was even angrier for my outburst, reluctantly drove the U-haul to Atlanta as I and my girls followed him in my car.

A month prior to the movie, I rented a car and drove to Atlanta for a job interview and to hopefully find an apartment. The interview was successful and they hired me on the spot. I met a couple of guys at the design conference (where I met my new best friend) and they offered me a job at a national magazine company in Norcross. The apartment I found was in the same complex my brother and sister (who shared an apartment) lived in. It was a beautiful apartment. High ceilings, crown molding, new appliances beautiful bathrooms… it was lovely.

When we arrived at the complex and finally dragged the last piece of furniture in, I couldn't help but sigh a long breath of relief. We made it. I finally left Oklahoma to chase a dream of being more and it was beginning to come true.

My oldest daughter was tested and placed in all gifted classes. My youngest daughter went to a local elementary school that she absolutely loved and it was in a beautiful place. Life was getting much better for all of us quickly!

On the first weekend I was in Atlanta, we went to visit our cousin and his family. We got to know one another sharing stories about our families, their kids were a little younger than mine, but we shared similar pasts. They were a lot of fun to hang out with and we had a great time. We'd smoked some weed together while there. Let's just say I underestimated the power and strength of the weed in Atlanta versus what I was used to back home. We left after midnight. My sister was with me and I should have let her drive. I don't know what I was thinking. We were getting on the highway to go home (my sister, kids and I) when as I turned to get on I-20 from the Lithonia exit, a woman in an SUV ran her stoplight, t-boning us as we got on the highway. The crash was sudden, hard and glass shattered everywhere. The SUV hit the vehicle on my sister's side of the car. The glass shattered in her face and she watched as the vehicle hit us head on. I could hear my baby daughter in the back seat screaming at the top of her lungs. My older daughter was silent and just as shocked as I was. I was frozen still. My sister was screaming. The owner of the SUV and her passenger, both of them black ran over to the car. They peered inside, eyeing each of us down. She looked at me and said, "I am so sorry, is everyone ok?" I looked around for the first time, silently praying everyone was ok. I looked at my sister and children.

Everyone looked ok… so, I said yes.

After that, all I could think about was my sister screaming my name and my baby girl in the backseat screaming at the top of her lungs, and my oldest screaming her nothing. My sister and daughter could have died. My sister was very angry. Before we got hit she kept saying, "Stephanie the light is turning yellow" but I reassured her (with my Oklahoma mentality on Atlanta streets) we had the right of way because their light couldn't possibly be green yet.

Everything replayed in my mind. I couldn't believe this. It was my first major accident and I didn't know what to do. My sister was on her cell phone with the police. That is when I noticed the driver and her passenger in that SUV ran back to the vehicle and drove off!

My sister began to yell at me to let her out. When I didn't respond, she climbed over me out of my car window and got out of the car. I was afraid as the police pulled up. I was sure I reeked of marijuana. My poor little car was severely damaged and my sister was extremely upset. My children calmed down after I reassured them but this unmistakably one of the worst incidents I'd ever experienced.

The policeman never mentioned the smell of marijuana on me, but simply stated, *"Welcome to Atlanta".* I didn't know then, but that would be an understatement.

My car wasn't totaled… I even drove it home. But it was so damaged that my insurance company kept the vehicle for about 5 weeks. In a lot of ways, it was good because it allowed me an opportunity to spend time with my brother every day.

At the time, my brother was driving a minivan. He allowed me to drop him off at work in the morning and then pick him up after because our schedules worked well that way. He was sacrificing for me. One night, he was angry at me. I can't remember why, but he came over my house to let me have it. He told me that the evening of the car accident, my mom told him that "now I was his problem to deal with" and that she didn't want anything else to do with me.

That night I vowed that good or bad, I would not call her anymore and grant her the peace of not dealing with me.

Love, Lust and Lifelong Friendship

My friend from Chicago came to visit me in my new apartment. At that time, I can say he has been the only man I ever felt an immense and almost hopeless romantic love for. Don't get me wrong. My husband loved me (I think it would even be safe to use present tense and say loves me) and I knew it, without question. But he had a hard time communicating his love for me.

Alternatively, this man who became my best friend, confidant, never judged and wooed me with his intelligence could easily communicate not only his thoughts, but most often had a clear perception of my thoughts as well. I must admit, I don't know if that was an indication of his experience in relationships, his intelligence or his ability to understand people but whatever it was, it was what I desired most. My love language is clear communication.

His visit infused me with passion, amorous love and joy. We had crazy in the xxx movies type sex everywhere. Countertops, floors, bathroom sink and shower… we did it. We drank as much of each other as we most possibly could. He was an insatiable lover. It was really all so new to me. I am not from Chicago and I really had limited experience with sex… so some of what he asked me to do had never been done and some of what I would attempt to do was a first try. It excited me to no end. I memorized every inch of his body like it was a map to ecstasy. I knew every crook, every scratch, the soft spots, the rough spots. He knew what to say, when to say it and how to say it.

Needless to say, I enjoyed his visit. He didn't stay long. It seemed to be our way. We could talk on the telephone for hours on end, but we couldn't be around each other in real life too long without fighting unless we were having sex. He was different. There were times when he was a bit reclusive and just wanted to be alone. I didn't understand it and I often took it as rejection. No matter what, we vowed to remain friends... always and forever.

Professional Ambitiion and Healthy Competition

My job was awesome. They were so flexible and accommodating. The company benefits far outweighed any benefits I received from ANY company in Oklahoma. It's an extremely conservative state.

At any rate, my new job was relatively easy to do and I really enjoyed it. I was a great artist and flipped my ads quickly. Because I was a supervisor before, I soon found I was up for a promotion. In order to receive the promotion, I was in competition with another young lady that had four years of seniority. Most of the employees in my department came from the Art Institute. She was definitely from the Art Institute. Because I came from a different market, I had a different eye for design and a different work ethic. I also approached management differently because my experience afforded me those gifts.

For a while it was really up in air as to who the promotion would go to. After a while, I just started believing God to do more and that I deserved the promotion. So after a two month wait, they finally announced that we were BOTH being promoted.

The Studio

In the interim, my brother was an artist, singing hooks on different tracks for local rappers. He went to the studio every weekend. They were good friends of his and he knew them for several years prior to my moving to Atlanta. On occasion, he would invite me to hang out with them.

The owners of the studio were a married couple. We walked in parallel universes. They'd been together as long as I'd been married so I understood a lot of what they went through. They had three boys that were the same ages as my girls. They were adorable in the sense that you knew they were madly in love with each other. He loved her with a grace that was unfathomable and she loved him in a way that was indescribable.

The studio was in the basement of their house and they were great people. It was a gorgeous home on spacious property. It became a second home to us. Maybe because they loved my brother, maybe because we just got along – I am not really sure, but we became one big family. My brother's best friends embraced me wholeheartedly and I still love each of them to this day, and I know they love me as well.

We spent most weekends there. Because it was a recording studio, they often had a lot of guests come in to record and collaborate. Our weekend routine was making sure the kids were good to go in their accommodations upstairs, making them food… finding out what they would be doing… and then heading downstairs to hang out or help out in the creative process.

The studio was always a safe place to have fun (especially as a single parent) because we never jeopardized the lives of our children by going out to party… it was our creative cave. A time when we could freely express everything we loved and hated about life.

I learned a lot about faith in God there. It was ironic because we walked close to the edge… did things we shouldn't have, often. I know church going folks would find it hard to believe but I learned the most about how good, forgiving and faithful God was from people who weren't supposed to be loved by God. Who weren't supposed to be able to teach about God, but even now looking back, had the best relationships with God. They were the relationships that depended solely upon Him and the truth of His promises, not in their ability to perform.

I always managed to always get "uplifted" in some way while I was there. We became a big family. My kids and their kids were great friends and enjoyed the time we spent there. All of them were like my brothers, his wife was my closest friend… We shared our talents and resources freely and often without question. We were unapologetic, unsanctioned, determined dream chasers. From helping to write music, to designing their album covers and reading my epic poetry, they fully supported my artistic talents. Atlanta became a land of art to me, a place where I could be free and celebrate me.

The couple in the studio would often buy me food to help feed my kids sending me home with arms full of groceries, words of encouragement and memories of fun, laughter and secrets we would keep forever. They fed me. I was literally fed in more ways than one. In a way, my brother took me to a place where I could heal and find healing.

We partied hard as most artists do. I could write a laundry list of things we tried to do, did and said that could probably get me arrested in 50 states! I always sobered up on Sunday mornings and would head home that afternoon. It became a way of life for me. It was my favorite activity and eventually, I hated to go home…

Time Alone

Home was a lonely place for me. It was a busy work week, taking care of my girls and just twiddling my thumbs waiting for the weekend. I would get so excited on Fridays. Some weeks I would just skip work on Friday to start the party early.

Eventually, I began popping pills (ecstasy). My first ecstasy pill was a birthday gift. I remember my little brother from Pennsylvania had just moved in with my brother and sister next door. My baby brother and I were extremely close and still are. I could relate to him and a lot of his frustrations. He and I were both looked at as the black sheep… and in our respective families, we were both the oldest. He was over my house when I took the pill. He looked at me and said, "I don't mess with that stuff." I remember thinking all was normal until I went into the bathroom. My first thought was, "Wow, these bathroom lights are brighter… and I look amazing!"

That day, I went and visited a friend in Edgewood. He was young, intelligent and a drug dealer I'd met through my cousin one weekend. I was 29 and he was 21. But he made a lot of money but was a product of the trap. The trap is your block(s) where you sell drugs. Often times, you don't get to leave that block because it is how you make your money. That's why they call it the trap… or at least that is how it was explained to me. He was a tiny guy with long dreads. He had pretty eyes and big lips. I loved to kiss him but would never do more than that. He was too young and he thought I was his ticket out and I didn't want to mislead him. That night, I went to see him and we talked and smoked weed all night. Which was our thing… it was what we did.

By the end of the night I'd told him about my birthday gift. He laughed and said, "Oh is that why you been on 10 all night?"

Reckless and Out of Control

About three weeks after the insurance company returned my car, I was headed to my cousin's house in Decatur. The magazine released us early on a Friday afternoon! I was so excited to start partying. I would just go and pick up my kids later… I remember singing that song, "The Pills, The Purp, The Coke, The Syrup?" (at least that is how I think it goes, I don't even know who sang it). I was so hyped up to finally relax.

Work, bills and debt were beginning to overtake me and add stress. The cost of living was high and I barely had enough to make ends meet. I called my then separated husband to discuss the kids coming to Oklahoma for the summer. He said something about not taking for the summer or only taking them for 2 weeks. Whatever he said made me upset and it surprised me. Next thing you know, I'd rear-ended a Surburban. The air bag deployed and acid from the air bag burned part of my face. Hot coffee flew all over the car. The phone sat on the floor as I tried to figure out what just happened.

I remember the Atlanta EMCare guy telling me my car was totaled. I didn't understand. He said because the airbag deployed, the car would be totaled out and I would need to get a new one. My face burned from the acid, my heart ached for my car and I all I wanted to do was get high.

Thank God for gap policies. My car was paid off and I went with

89

my brother to buy a new Toyota Corolla. It was a beautiful car. I had to take the car back to the dealer for them to add the tint. They gave me a loaner car. On my way to return it, would you believe I rear ended a person? Yes. It was a love tap... So, I drove off. I did. I was already ashamed about the other two accidents and I couldn't bear another.

I remember making it up to the corner and the bumper was like hanging a little. It was that plastic type of bumber. I popped it back into place and returned the loaner, vowing to be more careful. Technically, that was accident number three.

At work, I was the odd man out. Most of the group we worked with had been with the company for years and knew each other from days at the Arts Institute. I was a hardworking know-it-all, a single mom, black and a Senior Artist. We were over the other artists and considered their immediate supervisors. The other two senior artists would always lunch together and never invite me. I was a loner. Due to my authority, it wasn't considered politically correct to lunch with the artists, even though many were my friends.

One day, the woman senior artist that I was in competition with for the promotion was out and her cohort invited me to lunch. On our way to the Mexican restaurant, he asked that I stop at the gas station. Before he got out the car, he pulled out a corner of foil and sniffed from it. Then he went inside and bought a beer.

At that moment, I called my cousin. She was addicted to cocaine for a couple of years and always testified how happy she was not to be doing it anymore. I asked her if I should try it. She told me, I needed to make my own decision. I knew she should have said no and that I should have said no, but I was going to make my own bad choice anyway right? I've always wondered why she didn't just tell me to say no.

On our way to the restaurant, he drank the entire beer. Once we got inside, they'd barely brought the menus before he said, "I have something better than lunch".

Next thing you know we were headed halfway across town. We got to his apartment, which to this day, I can't tell you where it is. Once inside, he walked directly over to a plate in his kitchen. The plate had hills of cocaine the height of a pop can on it. There were three of them. He motioned to it as if to say "Help yourself."

I didn't want to seem timid or unsure, so I immediately walked over and did 3 long lines. All of a sudden, my stomach turned. I felt queasy. His brother looked at me and said, "Are you going to throw up?" I just walked into the bathroom and sat on the toilet. My mind was racing. I didn't expect this to be this way. It was cool and bad. I immediately felt "too" high. Suddenly, it dawned on me that we'd been gone for hours. I told him we needed to get back to work. I flew down the highways, so quickly that he was panic-stricken in his seat. The moment we walked in the building we saw our supervisor's supervisor's supervisor. Yes. The big dog. She took one look at us and laughed. I didn't know then, but this guy had a serious dependency problem. Because of his parent's money, great lawyers and such, there was little the company could do. They couldn't get rid of him because he admitted himself on numerous occasions to rehab and had admitted he had an issue. It only took that one time to get me hooked.

I loved cocaine. It became my drug of choice. Pills and marijuana took a backseat. I loved the process of breaking it down, making lines… doing them and starting over. It was almost as if I never had enough.

We were still going to the studio most weekends but I was in a different world. I still worked every day, did a ton of freelance graphic design and was writing more than ever… but coke became my best friend. It helped me to forget the absence of my Chicago friend, my messed up childhood, my ex-husband and the lack of support from my siblings. It made me forget that I was a single mom with two kids. All I did was draw, watch movies, get high and rest. I knew the coke was becoming a serious problem. Without it, I became angry and made poor decisions. On it, I was angry, made poor decisions and involved a lot of other people!

At work, the three of us senior artists became fast friends. We would bake biscuits (do lines) often during the workday. Then if I ran out of coke, I would pop pills. My weekends became weeklong activities and it soon got out of control.

Come to Jesus

One day, my brother and my sister took me on the balcony and had the come to Jesus talk with me. I was so angry at them. When I looked back at my life, I questioned whether God really loved me. I hated to think that God would allow me to get molested, allow a strange man to rape me, allow my friends boyfriend to die in front of me with a child on the way, that he would allow my ex-husband to lie to me and give me a sexual disease, that he wouldn't allow my Chicago friend and I to get along well enough to be who I was convinced we were meant to be… and that he would allow me to ruin my life with this drug problem. I was angry at him. All my life I felt like God was echoing with each situation that I wasn't good enough to have a good life. That I was supposed to be abandoned by my father, grow up poor, lose the only men in my life that ever loved me and be alone to deal with it all forever.

I was angry at them. I told them to leave and not to talk to me about God. But, in all honesty, they weren't the first to mention God or the most influential. The most influential person I talked to about God was the owner of the studios wife. She was a horrible alcoholic and an overt flirt with any guy that showed her more than a little attention, but she had a heart of pure gold and I loved her as a friend.

One day I was scared about my bills piling up and not being able to make it. We'd discuss me and the girls moving in at their house to help each of us on the bills, but she said, Stephanie… "Where is your faith?" I grew up in church, but I had no idea what she meant. She began to quote scriptures to me and explained the process and structure of believing in God. She told me the story of them getting their house and her lifelong dream of becoming a real estate agent. It made a powerful impact.

I remember picking up my bible and talking to God. I remember telling him, if there was anything at all to this book he'd better show it to me because I was ready to give up on life. I wanted to die, or to run away, or both. I hated myself. One night I knew I was going to get extremely high. I took 3 ecstasy pills and a quarter bag of coke. I prayed and asked God not to let it drop too heavy on me. This was a prayer I prayed often. I found myself sitting at the bottom of our stairway at 4 am without sleep, extra high. I felt like I was in some sort of prison. I couldn't stop if I wanted to. In that moment, I realized… I was an addict. I cried but it didn't make the high go away… nor did it make me want to live any longer.

Reading the bible was so brand new and I swear it was like each page I read was just for me. I began reading a little at a time. I started in Revelations but there was so much going on in that book that I had to take it back to the beginning. By the time I made it to I and II Kings, I was hooked. It taught me that GOD is true gangsta (no disrespect), meaning His word is bond. I could relate to that and even better, I respected that (remember communication and words are my love language). Everything he promises, he provides. Once I learned more, I shared more of what I learned with the world. I was not shy or remiss in sharing my thoughts and how this new found revelation was affecting my life.

That's when it began. My friends at the studio stopped inviting me. My brother reminded me they didn't want to hear about that bible or prayer or what I learned about Satan. As quickly as I'd made them, my new friends were gone. When my brother stopped wanting me around... they complied.

I was home alone. I felt sorry for myself. I was a drug addict. That is hard to accept when you work hard your entire life just to become something. It is hard to accept when you have little children looking up at you asking you regular questions about homework, school activities, etc.

I may have been learning to love God, but I was definitely teeter-tottering in that land that lies between this and that. So, I just prayed and I prayed often.

A New Friend

One night, I prayed that God would send me a good friend. I popped a pill and was beginning to roll. I wanted to keep my high up so I needed two things… a pack of Newports and Orange Juice. I went to the gas station up the street from my house. When I walked in, I immediately locked eyes with a really cute guy at the counter who was checking out. When I looked at what he bought, I couldn't help but smile. He was buying a pack of Newports and orange juice. But, I didn't say anything… I just went and got my orange juice. When I got to the counter, he was still standing there… staring at me. I laughed and asked, "What's up?" He smiled and said, "Yo, what up ma?" with a thick east coast accent. I can't remember how I ended up with his phone number but I talked to him all night that night.

He actually lived in an apartment complex right up the street from me. He came over my house the next night and we popped pills and watched a movie. I could tell he was digging me and I told him, "Everything that glitters ain't gold." He chuckled and said, "Don't I know it" or something like that.

From that night on, he and I became great friends. Eventually we had sex, but our relationship didn't revolve around that at all. Most often we didn't… we enjoyed being around each other more. Every time I talked to him he had a different job. It obviously wasn't his primary source of income. He always came over after 10 when the girls were in the bed asleep. I didn't believe in bringing men in my house around my kids ever. It was more about just having someone to come home to. He was super funny. I knew if he came over three things were certain. One, I would laugh my butt off. Two, we would watch a good movie. Three, I would fall asleep resting in his arms and he would be gone the next morning.

I don't know what he did when he wasn't with me but I knew he was doing a lot of dirt. We never talked about what he did outside of my home. When he came over it was all about watching a movie and relaxing. I just wanted him to hold me until I fell asleep and he didn't mind doing that. He would usually leave after I fell asleep and call me the next day.

When I told him about doing coke, we began doing coke together. He was so laid back. All he and I did was laugh and watch old movies together. No drama no mess. The only time I would get mad at him is when he didn't have any coke or couldn't bring me any. But, if he could… he would. We had tons of sex too (more like I was teaching him), but that isn't what it was about. It was different. I know God allowed him into my life and he came just in the nick of time. He never questioned my God talk and supported me. Years later, he told me that I came into his life at the right time. He said that he was a knuckle head getting into all sorts of trouble and that I was an angel in his life.

Truth be Told...

One day, heading home after a stressful day at work, I was looking down at my cell phone. I'd seen the light turn yellow but I knew I had time to make it. At work that day it was horrible, my supervisor was being a butt and picked on me and my artists despite our good work. By the time I had gotten to the stop light my bangs were already sticking straight up in the air from me pulling them that way, which is what I do when distressed. When I looked up the light turned red and from behind a bush to the right a car emerged in front of me. I knew hitting this woman was inevitable. I prayed to God with both hands in front of me and asked him to not let me kill this woman.

Our vehicles collided with such force, I thought I'd broken my leg and nose. My leg was pinched between the metal in the front seat of my car but not so much that I couldn't get it out. Shattered glass was all over my the dash, seats, my face and hands. No blood. I looked up to see the woman's car a couple of feet away. I didn't hit her directly, thank God. I'd hit her backseat, right behind the driver's side. She was crying and distraught. I was frozen in shock. I asked onlookers what happened and they indicated I ran a red light.

God granted my prayer...I didn't kill her. However, I did hit the woman with such force that I ruined her back for life. I remember the policeman asking me what happened and I just told him the truth. He remarked at my honesty. He said most people lied when placed in that situation.

My hand began to throb and hurt painfully. Evidently, when I'd lifted my hands up to pray, I cracked a bone in the lower part of my pinky because it hit the steering wheel with great force. As the paramedics wrapped my hand, my brother called and told me they couldn't find my kids. I began to panic all over again. My house was a wreck, my boss was a jerk, my car was totaled, and now my two daughters were missing.

As my brother and cousin arrived on the scene, my cousin looked at me and said something strangely profound. He said, "You are so blessed. You have no idea what a blessing this is going to be." I looked at him in bewilderment but never forgot his words.

My kids were with my sister. She'd picked them up and taken them to the store with her without telling anyone.

That night I was in the club with my brother and our friends, hand wrapped from wreck and all. Even though I couldn't do my hair with an injured hand, I still managed to look beautiful. My brothers friends were performing that night, so we'd all come together in support. It was the first time in a long time I'd seen any of them from the studio and we were happy to see one another.

At the club they always gave away a chicken dinner to whoever had the winning ticket. A person at our table won but didn't want to go down and get it. I said, "I'll go".

As I made my way down to the stage, they noticed my bandaging and asked about it. I announced to the club that I was in a wreck that day but God was good. I smiled really big and thanked them for my win. One of our studio friends laughed, stood up and shouted, "She is like that all the time folk!"

I Need Help!

After I totaled my new car, I was scared to drive and had absolutely nothing to drive. It would be a while before the Gap policy would kick in and I couldn't afford to miss work. I called my husband to come and help me. I demanded he come that weekend or that he shouldn't come at all. It was a couple of days after Valentine's Day. After my call to my husband, I called my friend in Chicago. He was upset I'd invited my husband back into my life, understanding what I'd been through before. I didn't tell my new friend about my husband coming back...

My husband rushed to help me. He left everything he had behind and came to my rescue. When he called to let me know he was up the street from my house my brother and I stood in my kitchen. He looked at me and smiled and said, "Are you ready for this?" I had to admit, I was beyond queasy. I had just finished reading in I Samuel how the children of Israel made a mistake of asking for a king as if God wasn't enough. It was if God had said the same thing to me. That I didn't need my husband to come and help me, but what was done was done and I would pay the price. My stomach turned.

When my husband arrived he was so happy to see me and the girls. He was different in a way. I knew he regretted letting our marriage fall apart and I have to admit I was a little happy to have a second chance at rebuilding our family.

Soon, my husband found a job at the local restaurant up the street. He allowed me to drive his car to work each day. Secretly, I was still doing coke. I would spend hours in the bathroom doing line after line. Then I would come out and talk to my husband. He was enamored at the woman I had become. I was more of a big city girl than ever. My hair was always fly, I was a size 6 at my biggest, kept my nails done, eyebrows arched and had a sassy attitude. Before long, my husband presented me with a ring he'd brought with him from home. He told me he knew we were only supposed to be friends but he wanted to be my husband again. Technically, he still was my husband.

I looked at that ring and all sorts of things raced in my mind. I was torn between this insanely fun life that I had decided to live and committing to my husband. I silently took the ring from him and slid it on my wedding finger. I smiled really big and hugged him.

One day we were supposed to head to the drive in to watch movies… but I had called my new friend to bring me some coke before we left. My friend was super late. He was upset about my husband moving in and I guess he should have been but we never established or named what we were… we just did what we did. I tried to reassure him my husband was there to help me and the girls and that was it, but once he saw the ring… he knew better. My husband liked my new friend. We all hung out from time to time getting high and laughing a lot.

Well, my friend was running late and I was flipping out. My husband and the girls were ready to go to the movie but I wouldn't leave. In fact, I was irate. I just told my husband I had something to tell him. It was important and was going to be crazy. I sat him down in our room and told him I was addicted to cocaine and was waiting on my friend to bring my stuff. That I couldn't go to the movies until he got there.

My husband was beyond understanding and insisted that he had done coke before in the past… that it wasn't anything new to him and that he wanted to do it too. Now, this pissed me off royally. I wish this was the part of the story I could say he was my knight in shining armor. Yes, he came when I asked. Yes, he brought the ring… but what kind of family could we be with he AND I strung out on coke?

After that, my friend and I grew closer. Rather than drive my husband's car, I would have him drop me off and my friend would pick me up from work. We would I do coke all the way from my job to my house, where he would come in and smoke weed with husband and I. My friend and I were once again the best of friends. We weren't sleeping together but we were able to keep enjoying each other's company and really, that's all we wanted.

Soon, my husband and I began to party like there was no tomorrow. We had several arguments. A month after he moved in, he wanted to pawn his car. He asked for the title and I promised him I didn't know where it was. He then somehow talked his mom into sending us a thousand dollars. The day he expected the money he demanded I give him the key to the mailbox. I denied it and he began punching me. He placed his checkbook between me and his fist so that it wouldn't leave marks. It reminded me o the day he bit my cheek when I asked him about bills. That was the day I hated bringing my husband back into our lives.

Now, both of our checks were going toward coke and what could be done about it? When my husband first moved in we tried to get his name added to my lease but because of his credit they wouldn't allow it. That was in June. A week before Christmas, they gave us a 7-day to vacate order. No warning. I thought it had to be because of something my husband did while I was at work. To this day it doesn't make sense. We paid our rent on time every month. I paid the rent, so I know. All I could think is that he slept with one of the red head manager in our complex and did something stupid to get us kicked out. I'd seen him flirt with the red head on more than one occasion.

With 7 days to vacate a week before Christmas, I had a serious come to Jesus moment. I remembered the principle of faith and all that I had been reading in the bible. (Yes, I was still reading then – in fact, I'd even started giving money to the church – just slipping it under the doorway. I would give an equivalent amount to whatever amount of money I spent on drugs that week... just to show God the drugs weren't a false god for me... I even got baptized... on September 16, 2007. I was high but I think the Holy Spirit whispered to that minister it was ok because I saw his hesitation and he did it anyway. My husband and kids were there to support me and watch).

I just chose to believe God had a place for us to go and that we would make it. We went to over 10 complexes trying to get an apartment with both of our names on it without luck. But, the first apartment I went to and tried to get on my own... I was accepted instantly – right there in the office. The complex was not only beautiful, it was less than 10 minutes from my job and the rent less than what we paid now. I loved it. Before long, my husband and I decided he had to leave. He went and got his own apartment not far from us.

Beauty and the Beast

That summer, DHS took his oldest daughter from her mother for some reason regarding abuse, a fire and some other stuff. I didn't get the whole story, just the parts he deemed were important for me to hear. He was working from 6 am to about 9 pm. She was 13, beautiful and headed down a path for trouble. I insisted my husband and she come live with us... that way I could keep an eye on her while he worked and we could split the bills.

She was a handful. She was demanding, even at 13. Her mother sent her with all of these clothes I would be embarrassed to wear as an adult. Tight shirts with the back out, high heels, short skirts and bootie shorts... no way was she going to wear that going anywhere with me or around my girls. There was no doubt she was already having sex. She flirted with grown men all the time and I know staying with us prevented her sub-sequential rape and pregnancy.

105

When God allowed us to find the new apartment, I was trying to turn over a new leaf. I began to read and study more… I even started going to a new church. My uncle invited us to a church he and my father were playing at one Easter morning. That day my oldest daughter told me she wanted to be baptized. So, we went back and never left. The head minister at that church was funny and very inviting. His family supported him and it was great to just be accepted and in church.

At the new apartment, I'd also been given one of those books by those people that walk around. Not the Jehovah Witness but the 7-Day Adventist. They offered to teach you bible study, so I filled out the card and said I wanted to learn more. Before you know it, one of those women was coming once a week to our apartment. The first day I met the bible study teacher, was a day my husband and I were arguing up a storm. The woman from upstairs had called him on his cell phone. How the hell did she get his number and why the hell would she be calling him? My husband was always one that didn't have to look far to find his mistress. I was beyond upset and angry. Here I was raising his kids and he didn't have enough respect to not flaunt his mess in my face. We were in the heat of an argument and he had just stormed out when the bible study teacher knocked on the door. I had been crying. I wiped my tears and asked how I could help her.

It was a beautiful night out, the sky was a pretty purple blue because the sun had just went down, the entryway to our apartment was near the back of the apartments and beautiful foliage surrounded us. She smiled, and said, "I received your card for bible study."

From that day forward, she provided me and my daughter's clear and concise instruction in the bible. I thank God for a spirit of discernment because when it was time to be invited into her "faith" God emphatically yelled NO in my spirit. I was to be non-denominational and believe solely in Jesus Christ and having a relationship with him. This is when I began to honor the Sabbath day. From Friday at sundown until Saturday at sundown we would worship God and rest from our work. It became a day of celebration for us. A time assigned for family, rest, worship and fun.

I Want to Live...

Several times, I almost overdosed. One memorable occasion was during a Sabbath. A coworker and I had scored earlier in the day... during our lunch break. We'd gone to the Art Institute to see what the new students were learning. Afterward we scored and got high on our way back and throughout the remainder of the day.

I remember asking the coworker that introduced me to coke how much was too much... I didn't want to OD. He said, no more than a

50 bag in an hour. I'd purchased a 50 bag that day, and that evening prior to the Sabbath I was almost out. From 1 pm – 5 pm, I'd done one bag... the bulk of it from 4 to 5, after work. By 5, I was calling my husband to score again.

He copped and by the time he got home, I was already in the zone... but he was ready to get there. So, we started doing lines back to back. I'd done so much cocaine my nose began to run uncontrollably. Tears were pouring from my eyes, slobber from my mouth. I couldn't talk. I stared at my husband across the room. I tried to scream for help with my eyes but he couldn't hear me. My heart was pounding so quickly. I lay back on the bed, panic-stricken. I kept thinking, "I can't die like this". No, I couldn't let my kids see me die like this. Above my bed, hung a bible study lesson I'd received at church. To this day, I can't locate the scripture, but it said that if I prayed and called on God to heal me, his angels would encamp around me... or something like that. I prayed in my heart as loudly and as strongly as I could. The heavy foot that hung over my heart began to lift, I could breathe, even talk. I was so relieved in that moment that God chose to save me. There was no doubt in my mind that the prayer and scriptures I'd recanted that hung on my wall saved my life that day.

I didn't vow not to use again, we still had half a bag left. But, I did stop that night. I promised myself that I would always honor the Sabbath and keep it holy from that point forward. And I have truly tried… not to a point of perfection, but I have tried my best.

I'd stopped using cocaine for a while. It had moments, you know waves. When you did a little, you couldn't help but do a lot… My heart melted the moment I realized I was going to use again. I had this painstaking feeling growing in my stomach for weeks prior to this moment. I knew it was coming. I knew it was going to happen. I just didn't know when. The terror and tears were back-building like the turbulent dark clouds of an impending storm about to release and set free multiple tornadoes that would damage the lives of many. My throat locked up. I looked at the ceiling in my room, my prison cell - only to avoid the tears that kept threatening to fall. "I don't want to do this. I hate this. I don't understand this feeling but I can't escape it. I need this and dang, I need it now." My thoughts fired off like bullets from a high-powered machine gun. I picked up the phone and called my husband. I pleaded with him to bring a bag of cocaine home with him from work. He tried to reason that we couldn't afford it, he tried to tell me we didn't need it, but who was he kidding. I knew he wanted it just as much as I did.

The Truth Hurts

I was sitting on my frumpled bed in front of a large bag of cocaine and my mind was saying no but my body was saying yes. A portion of the powder was sitting in the shape of a little hill on top of a large flat book with blue stars, a moon with an animated happy look plastered on its face, it was a children's book that I remembered was overdue to the local library. My 3 daughters were in the living room and bedroom of our small two bedroom apartment and my ex-husband sat across from me, staring intently. He looked at me with the same hunger for the drug I had. My stomach churned as I chop chop chopped. I carefully measured out 4 lines for us to snort. I looked for my half cut McDonald's straw... My body was geared up and ready to go. My mind was condemning myself and my spirit was praying to God that this time ended better than others. I just wanted to kick the clouds. But I also didn't want to. I wasn't confused, I truly lived in each emotional state, desire and hatred. They controlled me from day to day.

The truth is, my hands loved to chop up that coke and measure out lines that would give me the jolt I needed. The truth is I wanted to get high. I wanted to forget my cheating husband, overdue bills, a step daughter I couldn't control and a life I would seemingly never have.

I tried to quit. I tried to make this false god I didn't mind worshipping smaller and smaller. I would quit for weeks, but never really walk away in my mind... and this day, was day one of no longer clean… again.

Before long, I was reading and going to church much more often.
I took the girls each Sunday and became involved with activities.
I would help the culinary committee but the media committee
is where I shined. I designed the church website, twitter page
and made it possible for us to broadcast online… I was an active
member of our church doing whatever they would allow me to. I
was still using, but I was present and committed to a relationship
with the Lord as well.

Addiction is something that you mentally want to stop, but
often times physically can't. My body would crave the drug… but
only after something hit an emotional trigger. That trigger could
be perceived infidelity to competition with my daughter who was
gorgeous and wanted her father's attention, to a bad day at work.
Anything could push me over the edge it seemed.

When I would fall, I would repeat a scripture that always made
it better. "My grace is sufficient for thee, for in your weakness is my
strength made perfect." That scripture carried me from season to
season from binge to binge. Cocaine was by far the hardest obstacle
for me to overcome.

Remove the Mask

One Sunday, a senior pastor preached, "Remove the Mask". She was adamant about allowing the world to see the real you. It was the end of October and very near to Halloween. I remember that was the day after 3 months of sobriety that I chose to take the mask off. I went in deep. I spent over $200 on cocaine and had a never ending party. The family came to our house for Thanksgiving which was a joke. We'd been binge snorting for 3 days straight. By Christmas, my family members were asking if I was ok… but I wasn't. I knew I had a serious problem that only God could fix. During this 3 month binge, I had to leave work early one day due to cocaine just literally pouring out of me. Tears streamed my face, my nose wouldn't stop running… I'd taken pills and was paranoid. I finished my work within 2 hours and asked to go home. My supervisor refused. He was angry at me. I told him, I was sick and I was leaving. Period… it went well for me by the mercy of God because no repercussions resulted… but I'd definitely lost the respect of my peers and my artists.

When I got home from work that day, my oldest daughter, my husband's daughter lay next to me in bed. She hugged me tight and I told her that I was sorry. That they deserved better than me for a mother. That I should be the example of what to do and what not to do… I had a million of boxes of tissue around me… stuffed to capacity.

This is when I knew that I would love this little girl as though

I laid on the table and had her myself… she said. Mommy, we all make mistakes. You don't need to beat yourself up. It's ok. We love you and we are proud of you for all that you do. All, I could do was cry. She lay on the bed with me watching "The Gospel of Christ" for the rest of the afternoon. I will never forget that moment, at a time when she could have kicked me, she lifted me up. I will always remember that day.

Another day during the binge, I attended church with the girls. I didn't like to go when I was high but I needed desperately to hear from the Lord. I know it was obvious I was high because of how everyone looked at me. Despite their looks, I knew that each one of those members loved me. My pastor walked over to me and said, "Sister Stephanie, we want you to teach Sunday School." I looked at him like he was crazy… me? I smiled at him… deep inside, I love reading the bible and finding out what God is trying to say. I loved to share what I learned in my own life. I tried to reason with him, that I just couldn't do it and that he really didn't want me. But he insisted, and he said, "You need to start in two weeks."

And that is exactly what I did. I taught teenage girls. One Sunday, the group of girls (basketball players) came in and I could tell they were disinterested and trying greatly to disconnect with the lesson. We began to talk about forgiveness and what it truly means. We talked about it not mattering where you are today or were yesterday, even last night. That God is a right here and right now kind of God. That he doesn't care what everyone else thinks, it is between you and he and that is it. One of the girls broke down crying. She never shared what she was going through, but that it connected. When we got upstairs and opened the doors of the church, she gave her life to Christ. I was amazed. How and why would God use someone like me to bless and help others? I don't know.

Well, it was Christmas and I was high but I was also connected to God in a special way. I knew that he loved me in spite of me. We got to my father's house and a couple of people asked if we were ok. I responded yes, and one of my uncles asked me to pray. Again, God was using me but I didn't understand why. I prayed and afterward this spirit of guilt lifted off of me. My uncle had a way of letting us know that he loved us and cared for us. Even from a distance, I could always feel his love and that night was no different.

The night of New Year's Eve… I'd made up my mind. My youngest daughter decided she wanted to get baptized at the watch night service. I prayed to God that if my husband would too, I would quit doing coke forever. Can you believe my daughter got one toe in and backed out, but my husband got baptized?

It was amazing. I laughed at God for making my dream come true. Now, my entire family was baptized. That night was one of the hardest. As soon as we got back, my husband wanted to use. But I refused... despite the hunger in my bones to do so.

That night and many other nights after, I just prayed for Satan, to get thee behind me... and you know what? **That worked.**

Atlanta was a place of creativity, learning and growth. It also contained a lot of pain, confusion and bad choices. In it, I hear echoes of lost relationships, lost identity and God whispering, 'No more excuses'.

Chapter 7

A Mighty Battle is Never Won Alone

One day, I looked around the cluttered hallways I called my life and I was just tired. I stood in front of the stove staring at a step-daughter that hated me for discipline and questioning ways, a husband that hated me for the same and kids that had little respect for a recovering drug addict. Our bills were overdue, my husband and stepdaughter weren't on the lease and we'd just been evicted from our new apartment… and were technically squatters. To make matters worse, my husband was receiving calls from the woman that lived upstairs from us… and we'd only lived here 9 months. I just wanted to be free. I hated the path I chose and wanted so much more and so much better.

That's when it started… I began to sing those old hymnals I used to hear the senior women in our church sing during devotion when I was little. Standing in front of my stove, I was in awe that I remembered the songs and even the old ladies that sung them. These beautiful, weathered women would bellow from the gut in their stomach and you could almost hear it travel through their hearts to our ears.

"Lead me oh thy Great Jehovah, lead me with your powerful hand" and "I know it was the blood. I know it was the blood. I know it was the blood for me."

I could see them, standing proudly before a meager church body of early morning worshippers… They were physically weak, emotionally strong, spiritually seasoned and well understood what a life walking with Jesus meant. Freedom, faithfulness, trust, protection, unending love... they sang from experience and were not moved by words written in a hymnal with notes above. They sang from their hearts.

Now, I understood what those hymns meant! The words had meaning, life even. They began to echo in my heart, my head and my soul. They helped me in my darkest hours.

Those songs, reading the Bible and praying to Jesus saved me. I can tell you about all the cool stuff that I enjoyed like infidelity and drug use, and the amount of creativity that simply surged from me... but that would only be half of the story. The other half included fights (fights with anyone and everyone), loneliness, depression, self-hate, financial ruin, embarrassment, simply going coo coo for cocoa nuts and so much more.

During the period of time when I was transitioning from being me: the car accident having, lying drug addict to allowing Christ to live in me and through me wasn't a perfect path. It was littered with broken glass, tight walls to squeeze through and tight rope walks. Those hymns meant more to me in this place than anywhere else. They reminded me, I wasn't alone. Someone else, many in fact, have walked in a pair of shoes that were just like mine.

In the bible, it says we learn line by line, precept by precept. This is so true in my case. I can never judge or look down upon any person, because how could I possibly know where they are in their walk… or if they even started? God has perfect timing and his ways are far above my own. I sometimes I had to fall and get back up. At the end of the day, I learned one thing – Jesus NEVER stops loving us. NEVER.

Trouble At Work

My supervisor hated my new found love for Christ.

One day he asked me to join him in his office. As I sat across from him, I could tell he was guarded. I looked at the pictures on his desk… One of them was of his adorable red-headed son in a Halloween costume. Another was of he and his handsome husband. You could tell he loved them very much.

He began by saying, hesitantly, "I am an atheist." He went on to explain that he was raised in church and his father was a minister. His parents didn't approve of his lifestyle. In fact, they'd said some very hateful and hurtful things to him, attributing them to God and he in turn hated anything relating to God.

He reiterated that he was an atheist. I looked him in the eye and as gently as I could say it, I explained, "The God I serve loves everyone…" I wanted to explain that in life sometimes we were pushed to travel unmarked roads alone and that our relationship with Christ had to be our own and couldn't be narrated by anyone but the Father Himself… but I couldn't or maybe just didn't. He just looked at me with his big puppy eyes full of exasperation. He just wanted me to say "OK… I turn my love for Christ down". I didn't. I couldn't. Even if I wanted to turn it down, I couldn't. It's who I am – excited to do something new and must tell everyone I know Stephanie. I guess that is what irritated people about me. I wouldn't let things go. He dismissed me back to my desk.

Eventually, he targeted me for exclusion. He refused to acknowledge my successes and picked on my artists (making snide comments about how they were dressed, their sexual orientation, their design skills and more). He assigned me the lowest ranking artists despite my high scores or the turnaround in their scores once they were on my team. The other senior artists stopped hanging out with me for one, because I quit doing coke and for two, our supervisor made it obvious that he would not condone it. My team had the highest level of productivity and the fastest, most efficient turnaround times. Many of the sales persons were happy with our products and they often sent emails of praise our way.

One day, during our weekly meeting with sales reps, one of them asked if my supervisor shared a recent email he'd sent over. I replied no, this was the first I'd heard of it. I asked if he would forward it to me. He did.

Then the official attack began. In that company and any company I imagine, multiple write-ups justify termination. First, he wrote me up for not clocking out. The staff in our department shared an excel sheet on a universally located hard-drive to note time in and time out. On this particular evening, one of the other artists left it open… which in turn disabled me from clocking out. There was no way I could find out which artist left that sheet open and if they'd already left. There was no way I could ask them to close it so that I could clock out. I explained this to no avail and found it to be an unjustified write-up.

One of the things I loved most about working at the magazine was our quality assurance workflow. It worked as follows. 1) Sales rep or Client submits ad request via online portal. 2) Senior rep divides ads and assigns specific artists to ads. 3) Artists clocks in does ads and submits to QA (quality assurance dept.) 4) QA does spell-check and makes sure all written requests are complete. 5) Senior artist reviews ad again and either submits to sales reps for market or returns to artist for amendment.

We also had a clear set of rules on how to handle returned ads that required correction. Sometimes, we felt as though what was requested was completed as requested, other times there was a misunderstanding in communication. A situation like a botched retouch that needed to be redone fell squarely within that set. The rule was that if the need to readdress such ads fell after a specific time (5 PM) it would be tabled until the next morning. Well, the sales rep got upset because I knew the rule and exercised our rights to refuse the retouch until the next day. So, I got wrote up… again.

Two write-ups… at the rate they were coming, I felt as though I was fatefully headed for strike three which usually meant termination. I loved my work but began to hate the job. I wanted to quit so badly. In fact, I tried to. I attempted to e-mail my supervisor's supervisor but the email bounced back as if it were the wrong address. I opted not to go to work that day. No call, no report.

When I spoke to the woman that taught my bible study, she told me it was because God never intended for me to quit. The next day, (day two of no call no report) I prayed long and hard about it. That is when I felt God nudge me to write a letter to the Human Resources department. It was 5 pages long and titled, "A Gross Misuse of Power". I placed a copy of the letter on my supervisor's desk, his supervisor's desk and a final copy went to our Human Resources department.

The head of HR called. She courtly informed me that I needed to get to work if I wanted to keep my job and I needed to be there that morning. She was a close friend of the supervisors. I told her I could be there in 10 minutes. I asked her about the letter. She shortly answered that they would review it but I'd better get back into the office. I was saddened and felt defeated... she didn't give me the impression that she would read or investigate.

That morning, I'd read a couple of chapters in the book of Jeremiah. It spoke of him taking an important letter to the kings men. The king's men never gave the request to the king, in fact, they'd thrown it into the fire. After our phone call, I suddenly remembered we had a new president to the company. The president was adamant about being laser focused, a spirit of transparency and working for the good of the company. A document distributed to us had his e-mail address. I quickly e-mailed a copy of my Word file to him, expressed my concern that HR wasn't taking it seriously and got dressed to head to the office.

The document detailed specific situations that occurred during my tenure, including a time when I was up for a promotion with another department. The department head had an obvious crush on me. It didn't bother me in the least, he was harmless and just an overt flirt. I was excited at the opportunity to move up and work at a different office and increase my network of business friends. However, on the day of my interview, the head of HR required me to attend a mandatory meeting less than 45 minutes before the interview started. This would be great, except the interview was at the other building more than an hour away. She insisted it was mandatory and must be held BEFORE my interview. The meeting was about a sexual harassment claim my supervisor made against the hiring manager ON MY BEHALF. I calmly but assuredly explained that if I had a problem with him sexually harassing me I would have no problem making that known. I made it to the interview incredibly late and needless to say, I did not get the position.

By the time I arrived at the office, within the 10 minute window I promised (I lived five minutes away). I could tell the president had a clear discussion with the HR rep. Her attitude made a complete 180 turn and she assured me (in a way that said I know you tried to tell on me) they were going to look into the matter. Soon, HR demanded I provide them with proof for some of my claims. Not a problem. I was documenting every incident as they occurred. This is why I am an avid believer in a work diary! I backed my 5-page letter up with 11 e-mails and printed documents of saved instant messages sent over our Macs. It was how all artists communicated in the department and as a supervisor I always felt it was important to save those conversations in case I was ever questioned about what was explained. I additionally asked her to ask the other senior artists if I was lying or telling the truth. After a long day... later that afternoon around 5 pm, the HR director called me and asked that I come and see her.

She began the conversation with how much the company appreciated me and my hard work. It was clear by my work ethic, documentation, personal scores, and the scores of my artists that I was an excellent employee that they value. Then she went on to say that she researched my claims in the letter and that an apology was due to me. She talked to the other senior artists and they reaffirmed my claims. She gave me a gold envelope with a case discovery letter inside. Inside, the letter indicated the supervisor was to provide an apology in the presence of his supervisor.

I was a hard worker and did a great job. I valued my work and prayed each day to do an excellent job. Even when I stumbled and fell into a bad place, I provided consistent work and always pushed my artists to do an excellent job.

On the flip side, the letter in the gold envelope was duped. The supervisors name was misspelled at every opportunity. The apology he was supposed to give in the presence of his supervisor never happened. I got pulled into the office and we all sat and looked at each other. The apology never transpired. But, needless to say, I was happy. I wasn't going to get fired over some non-existent mess and it was obvious, I would never have to worry about mistreatment from him again. He was crushed and rightfully so.

To this I owe and attribute it all to God. I thank God that I prayed every day in that building. That I was committed to doing an excellent job and that he protected me and guided me when the time was right. His Word taught me not to fight and to trust HIM to fight my battles and boy did he come through.

Later that week, they had a meeting for managers about, "How NOT to treat your employees". Obviously, they made it known in that meeting who did what and how... to some degree. One of the other managers came to me and asked what I did because whatever it was it was powerful. Soon, some of the best artists in our group were transferred to my team. A lot of the artists didn't know what was going on because I wasn't vocal about being upset. I was just quiet and thoughtful. I have always been that way. I prayed every day at that job for God to send someone to recognize my hard work or if he would please send me to a job that appreciated me.

Within a couple weeks a new supervisor was hired and I was transferred to work with her. She was cool but I felt like my tenure with the company was over. I probably could have worked there another 10 years without issue... but it was time to move on.

Just Me... and the Girls

When I made a solid decision to stop partying and commit my life to Christ my ex and I came to an impasse. He was upset and we began to fight about money and everything else. Eventually he moved out and later moved back to Oklahoma. His oldest daughter stayed for a while after he left, but eventually also moved back to Oklahoma. It was the hardest time because I was turning over a new leaf, learning to depend solely on Christ and my money was a mess. I remember sending the kids to Oklahoma for the summer and the week they left our water had been shut off due to non-payment. At the time, I was paying a mortgage, car payment, insurance, electric, phone bill and more. My paychecks only covered the rent and the car payment. All the other I had to hustle my graphic design to get.

I remember telling one of the senior pastors (the remove the mask pastor) about my water. She lived down the street from me. When I say, I love this woman to pieces, I do. She was amazing. She could read me like an open book. It was no use hiding anything from her because if I didn't volunteer it she would ask until I shared.

One thing I know. As a single mom, you don't want people to know the struggles you face. It bears a lot of shame and it tears at the fabric of your self-esteem. You want others to assume the best and hate the thought of sharing how horrible and tragic it might actually be. Most often, we suffer in silence and deteriorate from the inside out… becoming bitter women and hateful to the world that surrounds us.

This woman, who was married for many years and had 6 adult

children of her own would let me come down to fill water jugs and make me gallons of koolaid to take home with me. I hated to bother her so much. Who knew as a woman living on your own you needed so much water. But you need water to bathe, use the bathroom, wash dishes and drink. I remember going to the Pickneyville Park up the street from my house to steal water. I would take 4 to 5 2-gallon jugs and just fill those puppies up. It was hard for me. Once, when I arrived at the park, I saw two people in black watching me. I just knew they were park authorities so I abandoned my water mission and baled.

I had horrible toothaches then too. The kids were gone, it was just me in this big house... and my mouth was swollen. I was in so much pain. I remember the side of my face was literally the size of a baseball. I couldn't afford to go to the dentist. All I could do was press a warm washcloth against my chin and pray it went down.

I spent most evenings in the family room. The girls and I spent most of our time in my huge bedroom and being up there made me think of them. So, I pretty much stayed downstairs in that family room.

One night, I began to sing. I had a habit of playing these old records I'd found in the garage of the house. My favorite was John P. Kee. Even though my jaw was huge, I sang along, "I will trust in the Lord. I will trust in the Lord." I couldn't sleep for the pain. After I sang, I sat down and wrote, "The Harmony of Determined Feet".

It was an epic poem of a teenage girl that left home for the big city. She loved the fast life and fast men and eventually became a stripper. One day at the mall, she met a guy that changed her life. He was a drug dealer and had tons of money. She began to live with him and soon became a drug addict and a prostitute for him. She finally decided to quit and ran away. But she discovered soon after she was pregnant. She was still a crack addict, homeless and pregnant but her boyfriend couldn't stand the thought of her running away. She had the baby and thanked God for a healthy baby. She was still homeless finding shelter here and there. Well, she'd somehow found a place but the pimp found her too. He was furious with her and in his fury he ended up killing the baby and her too. The story ends with him in prison facing the death penalty on his last day of life. He and she found God prior to death but not before the consequences of their life choices had determined their fate. It was an amazing poem.

Moving to DC

I'd been volunteering at a local Christian TV station in Atlanta for about 7 months. I'd go every Tuesday working in their prayer room on the prayer line. There were regular callers that prayed every week with you but every now and again, you would get a call that let you know, having your water turned off or not making your car payment on time weren't big deals. A lot of older people would call in with health issues, or just wanting to be reminded that God still loved them. One young man called. He was in his 20's... he and his son were living beneath a bridge because they lost their home.

This taught me that people are always suffering and there is someone that needs reassurance every day that God cares.

This work moved me and inspired me to begin a prayer ministry. I printed several business cards with unique sayings and started my work. I purchased an additional phone line on my phone and waited for the phone to ring. It never did! No matter how many cards I handed out I didn't get one call.

I decided moving to DC would be great for me. I would take the prayer ministry there and start a new chapter in my career. On my budget, moving to DC basically meant living in Baltimore or Virginia... I chose Virginia. It seemed safer and the schools appeared to have a positive environment for the girls.

Moving was scary. But, I was being obedient to what I felt God was directing me to do. I put in my notice at the magazine, cashed in my 401K monies (about $10,000) and began looking for a place to live. I remember not having my money for the house payment that month and just waiting on that check to come in.

We moved all of our furniture into a storage unit, packed what we could in our car and headed for DC. Our destination was an extended stay hotel. When we got to the hotel (after a 12 hour drive from Atlanta) and it was lackluster and small. There was one queen bed and an armchair. There was a refrigerator and desktop stove, TV with minimal cable and free wi-fi. All for the super low price of $998 a month. The cheapest apartments in Virginia ranged from $1,400 per month to about $2,200 per month. I knew the lowest salary I could take was around $50K based on the cost of living alone.

Days were long and tiresome. I searched and searched, interviewed and interviewed without success. By November, I was forced to take a temporary job with an online shopping center. The store was a massive and an efficient machine. The more people began ordering for the holidays, the more intense and longer my schedule was. It was a 4 day on, 3 day off schedule, with 12 hour shifts. I was packing boxes. I worked hard for those shifts that spanned from 6 am – 6 pm. It took about 45 minutes to get there. So, work was 14 hour days with minimal pay. I was dying inside.

Many nights I awoke with pain and muscle spasms in my hands. I cried out to God wondering what he was doing. I cried and told him that using my hands was how I made money. I could almost hear God laughing… and sympathizing with me. You see, soon I realized that God had a greater plan.

By Christmas, I was out of money. My oldest daughter's birthday falls 3 days after Christmas and I was sorely depressed. I cried and cried to no avail. It was hard to wear the everything is ok hat with a 14 year old and a 10 year old looking up to you each day. The best part about it all, was having time off to spend with my daughters. This was the most time I'd ever spent with them as I was always working, busy or pre-occupied with my own personal agenda. This period of time required me to slow down, pray, study and learn more about myself and my relationship with God.

By New Year's Day, my car was packed and I was headed home… back to Oklahoma. My mother in law Western Union me the funds I needed to get back home, but only if I promised to stay…

In this season of my life… during every hardship and every turn, I felt the echo of God's presence walking with me and never leaving me alone to "figure it out". Every battle I had to fight, it was He that wielded the sword.

Chapter 8

Happily Ever After...

I came back to Oklahoma with a realization that all the demons I tried to run from ran with me. There was never a reason to run from my truth and there was no escaping it. Trying to escape, cover and hide only led me down a path that created more trouble and invited death to my doorstep a million times over. The fact is we will face a lot of trouble in life. We will have trouble that we invite and manage from a place of comfort and trouble that hits us without our invitation or decision.

But in the end, we also have Jesus. I know the whole Jesus thing seems overrated. I mean, we hear our relatives talking about how good God is but we can't see it with bare eyes. It's not until we actively seek a relationship with Christ that we begin to understand this. I know reading the Bible opened up something inside me. But, in reality, I didn't have any other place to go. You see, I played my hand to the best of my ability and I ended up lost and confused. But when I gave up my idea of what life was supposed to be, he gave me beauty and peace.

If you really try Him at His word I promise you won't be disappointed. People disappoint. People lie. People steal and misuse your trust. We are only human, and by nature we are imperfect.

But, God will only earn more and more of your trust as you begin to allow Him to.

Do hard days come? Yes. Will they stop? No.

This morning I woke up with my current troubles on my mind... Visually and better stated literally, some situations look hopeless. In an instant, I heard, "Perfect love casts out ALL fear". I embraced it in my spirit. I decided then and long ago, that I would no longer let my situation or my emotions depict how I perceived my today to be. My today is always good because I wake up in and under the loving protection, grace and direction of God. In this way, the scripture, "This is the day the Lord has made and I will rejoice in it" becomes a strong cup of tea that is easy to sip.

Here's the reason I was willing to share my pain, my past and my personal experiences with you... I want you to know you can still PUSH FORWARD into YOUR PURPOSE!

I am Still Here!

Being molested, seeing a friend murdered, having another commit suicide, rape, not one but six car accidents, two overdoses, losing my grandpa's and a great uncle, one long loving then tiresome marriage, adultery, homelessness and hopelessness and I am still here!

I didn't commit suicide. I didn't die. I didn't murder anyone and I haven't been to jail. The grace of God covered me in my mess, through the mess others dragged me through and into a victorious and trusting life filled with an unending love I could never pay for.

No matter what I do, I can't earn it, don't deserve it and wouldn't begin to know how to pay for it.

The only thing I can do is try to love Jesus the way he loves me by walking in my purpose. Unconditionally… not pointing fingers at Him and screaming why, not blaming him for my poor choices, not blaming him for the poor choices of those I chose to trust and love but instead, I can love him back in obedience. No, I will not be perfect but I can certainly try my best. When (not if) I fall, I know his grace is sufficient enough to get back up and keep running the race.

What echoes in my spirit is that many think the gift is eternal life in Heaven. NO. The BONUS is going to Heaven. The GIFT is a peace filled life leaning and trusting in Jesus.

Chapter 9

Echoes

Even when you walk with God, you have to wake up each morning and live with you, the "you" that resulted after life's choices and mishaps, the "you" that remains and moves forward each day, the "you" that you may see as inadequate and unworthy... and what in the world do you do with "you"?

First things first, turn off those negative voices that say you have failed in life. No you haven't. You have lived the life that leads to your purpose. No matter how crazy or ugly it may be, it's yours. Embrace it and cherish the lessons it afforded you.

Echoes Can Haunt You If You Let Them

Whore. When I was young and realized by age 12 I wasn't a virgin, I thought it meant I was a whore. Even though I'd been molested, I connected with the identity and wore it internally each day.

Thug. I hung out with gang bangers and thugs and I loved it. I was bad and I condoned bad behavior. I was a thug and I wore it like a badge of honor.

Murderer. I had an abortion and I killed what would have been my second born child. I killed a person because it would have made my life inconvenient. How could I live with myself?

Horrible Wife. I drove my husband away by not giving him what he wanted. I left him many times and even turned to other men to carry me through my pain.

Reckless. I was a reckless driver and almost killed my sister, another woman and myself. I invited a strange man to my home and he raped me. What kind of person can't drive? What kind of person meets someone on the internet and allows them into their home?

Drug Addict. This one I wore for at least 15 years of my life. I thought it was cool and a great way to solve my problems. But when I sobered up the problems were still there and I just wanted to get higher.

Horrible Mother. My poor kids... not only did I live a selfish life, but I was the worst role model. How could I ever expect them to love me?

Workaholic. I work all the time and love to work... how can I possibly have a life if all I do is work? I will never be socialite or accepted.

Un-dateable. I can't keep a good relationship. Every man seems to run from me or away from me. What's wrong with me?

Fatherless. I used to feel like my dad didn't love me. I took his absence and indifference as a reflection of his true emotional state toward me. I felt unwanted and unloved.

As a mature adult looking back this list is bullshit (excuse my language). It's not as if it isn't natural to beat ourselves up. It is. But, just because it's natural doesn't mean it's ok or right. All of these

141

things are just events along the journey of my life and influence the decision making person I am today.

It's ok to make mistakes. Some of us don't have the luxury of making mistakes no one else can see. If you are one of those lucky people, it is time to stop beating yourself up for yesterday and to start chasing your tomorrows. But what you have to know is that it's not what everyone else whispers behind your back that bears the most weight, it's what you have convinced yourself you are or aren't that is most important. *It's the whispers you allow to echo in your own mind that will kill you.*

I know you learned a lot in those bad choices just like I did. I learned life's most valuable lessons in the school of hard knocks. Nothing anyone could tell me would teach me and I had to learn in my own way… I think those are the lessons that stick with us most.

As you look in the mirror of your life, what do you see? Do you see a reverbing reflection of your past? Do you see the times when someone who was supposed to love and protect you but didn't and instead they hurt you? Do you see patterns of abuse exemplified in your actions toward others or self? Do you see a life of wasted time being selfish? Do you still hear the footsteps of every strong influential man or woman that has walked away in life? If so, it is time to change what echoes you allow to reverb in your life.

I dare you to write the lies down and then cross each one of them

out. When I wanted to move forward, when I dared to dream…
every time hope wanted to bless me, my past threatened me.

What Echoes in You?

Get dirty. Write your list. Stop ignoring it, confess it, renounce it
and thrive. You might as well write them down now and get it out
of your system. As you do, you will begin to heal.

When I Refused to Let Go

When I refused to let go, *I chose excuses over change.* Instead,
I would let mistakes and the events play like a broken record,
constantly justifying why I couldn't do more or be more.

I used to hear and see painful images of me being molested. They
seemed to bother me more as an adult than when I was a child. It
was as if those memories served as a mile marker etching a path to
self-hatred.

*Now those memories serve as a testament of strength and
perseverance.*

I remembered being a gang banger and choosing to do drugs
and party with friends instead of pursuing education and my
future. I would see a picture of someone lost and stupid. Someone
overdosing on a bed or too high to even understand what was going
on around her.

143

I had to learn life's hard lessons in order to SERVE in a future I couldn't imagine.

I used to see the arguments, the cheating, the lies and financial burdens of marriage. I would see a woman who couldn't hold on to her marriage.

I face the fact that some relationships are only for a season and they organically change over time.

I was afraid to drive for a while. I didn't trust myself to make good decisions behind the wheel. I felt reckless and unsure of myself. *I know... this is life or death and I CHOOSE life.*

As a mother, I felt like an epic failure many times over: failed marriage, drugs, abortion, workaholic – you name it, it all equated to being a bad mom.

I realize that my transparency and fortitude helped to teach my kids about life in a way that a school book, internet or movie couldn't. My ability to overcome and persevere alone and still make it says I am stronger than any bad choice I could ever make. It has allowed me to be a real mother connecting with my kids on a level most parents are afraid to walk on... a level of truth and sincerity.

I love to work and it is an area I have yet to fail in (in my opinion —insert laughter). So, my obsession with work was insatiable. I wanted to work and make money all the time. It was all I could think about. But, it was driving me away from my family and placing me in denial in every other area of my life.

I understand that work is a vehicle that allows my family to live safely and securely in a society that requires money in order to survive...it is simply a means of survival and not my identity.

Being a single parent, you must assume a lot of lonely nights. But, being a celibate single mother ensures you will spend many nights alone. Setting standards for who is allowed to be in your life or a part of your life isn't easy and if you second guess yourself you will compromise. Who you decide to introduce your children to is a serious matter. At one time, I thought this meant I was un-dateable. Loneliness would consume me and try to convince me I was worthless. I laugh at this now, because it means so much more.

I realize that not only am I dateable but I am a great catch. I won't ever be good to a lot of people, but to a special person, I will be amazing and wonderful. That is good enough for me! I like the thought of having someone that is hand-made and tailor fit by God just for me. I know that when the day comes (as I am positive it will) this person will bring immense happiness and joy in my life and I will laugh a whole lot!

Most importantly, I used to feel tremendous pain at the loss of the most influential men in my life. I could hear their footsteps echoing down the hallway of my life... leaving me forever. Growing up without my father's overt love and affection caused me to value and cherish the love of the caring men in my life. My heart broke a million times over at the loss of my grandfathers, my Uncle Jr., my ex-husband, my best friend in Chicago and the many friends I had to separate from as I chose a life of sobriety… they each helped me to become the person I am today. I used to internalize their loss of love or absence as a reflection of my person…

Today, I am immensely thankful for hearing the melodic steady and consistent life-giving heartbeat of what remains… the pulse of Jesus that rests in me, around me and through me blessing my life and those I come in contact with. His life-giving Words refresh my soul and echo harmoniously with my spirit. Every morning I awake with a peace and expectancy I can't describe as anything less than happiness because I **CHOOSE** *to listen to the good and not the bad.*

About the Author

Stephanie D. Moore is the mother of three beautiful girls.

She loves to work with the community to create programs that inspire change. She has created and served several groups including: KYSE—Kiss Your Self-Esteem, a program dedicated to helping women overcome life's obstacles and move forward into purpose; She's a BOSSE—A Beautiful Oasis of Success, Style and Elegance - a group dedicated to helping teen girls learn more about health and wellness, beauty, etiquette and self-esteem; and Grindaholix—Young Men on the Rise, a group dedicated to encouraging young African-American men by way of mentorship and learning from leaders in the community as it relates to entrepreneurship, leadership, spirituality, responsibility, finance and fatherhood.

Stephanie is also the owner of Moore Marketing and Communications, a design firm housing several brands including ThatPRChick—Public Relations for Personal Brands; Apes, Peacocks & Ivory—Graphic & Web Design Firm; MooBackwards—Social Media & Online Marketing Firm; Branding IS Strategic—Blogging Platform sharing key content on marketing, advertising, branding, social media and public relations; and His Broken Voice—Blogging Platform dedicated to sharing content on diversity in television media.

Stephanie has worked in various traditional media (television/ print/web) forums for more than 10 years. She now resides in Oklahoma City. Oklahoma City is a Nielsen #41 Market.

Made in the USA
Lexington, KY
26 March 2015